Bedtime Stories for Girls of Destiny

45 Tales of Extraordinary Latter-day Saint Women

Written by
Raeleigh Wilkinson

CFI · AN IMPRINT OF CEDAR FORT, INC. · SPRINGVILLE, Utah

"to the WOMEN who iNSPiRE ME AND the GiRLS WhO WiLL ChANGE the WORLD."

-RaeLeigh

Text © 2022 Raeleigh Wilkinson

Artwork © 2022 Brooke Bowen, Esther Candari, Sarah Hawkes, Victoria-Riza Hyde, Samantha Long, Brooklynne Noe, and Ellie Osborne

ISBN 13: 978-1-4621-4182-1

Library of Congress Control Number: 2022935433

Published by CFI, an imprint of Cedar Fort, Inc.
2373 W. 700 S., Springville, UT 84663
Distributed by Cedar Fort, Inc., www.cedarfort.com

Cover design and interior layout and design by Shawnda T. Craig
Cover design © 2022 Cedar Fort, Inc.

Printed in the United States of America

10 9 8 7 6 5 4 3 2 1

Printed on acid-free paper

This book belongs to

Contents

Artwork

Samantha Long

Brookynne Noe

Ellie Osborne

Aïda Stevenson

1936–
Spain and France

ONCE UPON A TIME, there was a little girl who could draw before she could walk. In her native country of Spain, Aïda spent hours sitting on the sun-warmed pavement drawing with chalk. When Aïda was only three years old, she and her mother fled to France because of the Spanish Civil War. They found safety in a refugee camp in Toulouse, France. One day, a French couple who had always wanted a daughter invited Aïda and her mother to stay in their home. The French man told Aïda's mother that his wife had also always wished for a sister, so Aïda and her mother were welcomed as family.

On her first day of school in France, Aïda was overjoyed with her desk full of crayons and paper. She loved to sing and play with her new classmates, but mostly she loved stories. In no time at all, Aïda was reading and writing in French. When her father escaped from Spain a year later and joined the family, he made it his mission to also teach her to read in Spanish.

When it was time for Aïda to go to college, she decided to study painting. After she graduated, Aïda and her sister traveled to Switzerland to teach French. One day, Aïda saw a sign advertising an English class. Aïda had always wanted to learn English, so she and her sister attended the class. There, Aïda met the missionaries from The Church of Jesus Christ of Latter-day Saints. The missionaries began to teach her about the gospel, and she welcomed their teachings into her heart. "When we pray, we can speak to Heavenly Father," the missionaries said.

"I know!" said Aïda. "I speak to Him every day!" Aïda was soon baptized and spent much of her time helping the missionaries until she met her husband.

While Aïda raised three children, she taught French, painted, and wrote and illustrated children's books. "We are, above all, creators," she said. In her later years, Aïda lost most of her sight, but she still found happiness in a summer breeze and the tiny footsteps of her grandchildren. She said, "Even if I could no longer write, if I could no longer speak, I could always hold others in my arms."

Anna Karine Gaarden Widtsoe

1849–1919
Widtsoe, Norway

ONCE UPON A TIME, *there was a woman in Norway who received a secret message in a shoe. The message was about the restored gospel of Jesus Christ, and it came from shoemaker Johnson of Trondheim.*

"What is the meaning of this?" Anna asked.

"You may be surprised to hear that I can give you something more valuable than soles for your child's shoes," the brave shoemaker replied.

Anna was curious, but when she heard that he was a "Mormon," she bolted from the shop, horrified. There was strong prejudice in Norway against this new religion, and Anna was a well-educated and respected widow of an accomplished teacher with two sons to support. She couldn't have her community turn against her! Nevertheless, Anna's curiosity eventually led her to a meeting in the upper floor of the shoemaker's house, where she gained a testimony of the truth of the restored gospel. On a chilly April day after many months of searching and pondering, Anna was baptized in the icy Trondheim fjord. Despite the Arctic water, Anna felt nothing but warmth.

After Anna's baptism, she was banished from her community and rejected by her family. Although she was hesitant to abandon her homeland, her sister Petroline, and her husband's grave, she longed to join the community of Saints in Utah and enter the temple to be sealed to her husband. Anna gathered her courage and made the long journey with her young sons to Logan, Utah. In Utah, Anna ensured that her sons received the best education possible. Some of Anna's neigh-

bors questioned her commitment to their schooling, but Anna was determined that her sons' education would be a tribute to their father's life's work. Anna's sons both became university presidents, and her oldest son, John Widtsoe, became an apostle.

Anna was sealed to her husband by proxy on a joyful day shortly after the Logan Utah Temple dedication. To add to her joy, her beloved sister, Petroline, joined the Church in Norway and announced her plans to immigrate to Utah. Anna, missing her homeland dearly, asked Petroline to bring as many Norwegian flowers as she could.

A few years later, Anna and Petroline returned to Norway together as some of the first single sister missionaries in the Church. They served together for four and a half years, preaching the gospel and destroying the rumors that had previously made Norwegians suspicious of the Church.

Anna lived the rest of her years in Utah with her sister, tending to her flowers, writing beautiful poetry in her native Norwegian tongue, and cherishing her grandchildren. Before she died, she told her son, "The most glorious thing that came into my life was the message delivered to me by shoemaker Johnson of Trondheim. The restored gospel has been the great joy of my life."

Astrid Tuminez

1964–
Philippines

ONCE UPON A TIME, there was a hut with holes in the roof where a little girl named Astrid lived with her family. Astrid's family lived in one of the poorest slums in the Philippines. When the night sky was clear, Astrid gazed up at the stars and wondered what she would do with her life. "Dreams are free," she would remind herself.

When she was five years old, Astrid's world changed forever. Nuns from the Daughters of Charity visited Astrid's family and offered Astrid and her sisters a free education. Astrid and her sisters were thrilled! But on the first day of class, Astrid was placed in the last seat of the last row—the seat reserved for the worst student. Throughout the year, she spent recess in the library devouring *Time* magazine, Nancy Drew, and Dr. Seuss books. By the end of the year, Astrid made it to the first seat of the first row—the top of her class!

The missionaries found Astrid's family when she was ten years old. As they taught her about the plan of happiness and her potential as a daughter of Heavenly Parents, she felt like she was looking through her roof at the stars again. It didn't matter where she came from; she had unlimited potential. The missionaries asked Astrid what she wanted to be when she grew up, and she quickly responded, "I will work in New York City for the United Nations!"

Astrid received a scholarship to attend the University of Manila, but she had her sights set on an education in the United States. After her first year at university, during which her sisters worked and saved to help pay Astrid's tuition, she received a full scholarship and graduated as the valedictorian of her class with a degree in Russian literature and international relations.

Astrid was concerned about nuclear weapons and the Cold War with Russia, so she decided to pursue a master's degree from Harvard in Soviet studies and a doctorate degree from the Massachusetts Institute of Technology in political science. Astrid worked as an intern at the United Nation, achieving the goal she set as a ten-year-old girl. She then became a world leader in both political science and technology. She was an executive at Microsoft, where she led corporate, external, and legal affiars in Southeast Asia. In 2018, she became the first female president of Utah Valley University. In each of her leadership roles, Astrid remembered to see Christ in everyone—a lesson she learned from the Daughters of Charity.

Astrid also advocates for the empowerment and education of women. She said, "Women are ready to do more and be more. We can be engineers, mathematicians, business people, educators—or whatever else we dream of being."

Caroline Kwok

1952–
Hong Kong

ONCE UPON A TIME, in Hong Kong there was an eight-year-old girl named Caroline standing by the side of a swimming pool in a white jumpsuit. It was Caroline's baptism day, and she was so thrilled she could barely keep herself from jumping into the pool. She loved singing and learning about the scriptures in Primary. In fact, Caroline loved to learn about anything!

When Caroline grew up, she decided to attend the Church College of Hawaii (now BYU—Hawaii) for her undergraduate education. She spent many late nights at the library, and despite her friends' invitations, she didn't spend time or money on any activities for which she wouldn't get a grade.

One day Caroline rushed into sacrament meeting while the congregation sang the opening hymn. As she paged through the hymnbook to join the singing, she heard the voice of the Spirit whisper, "Caroline, go on a mission." Caroline was surprised, but she decided to follow the prompting. However, when Caroline called her mother and told her about her desire to serve a mission, Caroline's mother told her not to go. Caroline hung up the phone and put her head in her hands. Caroline's upbringing in China had taught her to honor her parents, but the Spirit had been so clear. Should she listen to the Spirit, or should she listen to her parents? Caroline decided to follow the Spirit, and she served a mission.

When Caroline returned to Hong Kong after she finished her undergraduate degree, she wasn't sure of her next path. As she considered the leaders in the Church in Hong Kong, she noticed there were many leaders with business and finance degrees but no one in education at the university level. She decided to pursue a PhD in education. Caroline's expertise in education led her to open a night school for Church members who worked during the day but wanted to further their education. Caroline created a curriculum that covered both secular knowledge and gospel principles, helping her students increase their testimonies and their knowledge.

"The power to progress and grow is in each one of us," Caroline said. "We just have to gain access to it with the Lord's help and with belief in our own abilities."

Reeve Nield, Laurette Maritz, Cecilie Lundgreen
1967–   1964–   1973–
Zimbabwe, South Africa, and Norway

ONCE UPON A TIME, thirteen-year-old Reeve was finishing a tennis lesson with her father in Zimbabwe. He said, "Now, Reeve, be sure to share everything you have learned with others." As Reeve grew up, she mastered many sports and increased her testimony. At every opportunity, she shared both her sporting and spiritual knowledge. Reeve's favorite sport was golf, and when she grew up, she became a professional golfer and golf coach. One woman she trained was named Laurette Maritz (but everyone called her Lolly). Lolly became one of South Africa's top lady golfers and one of Reeve's closest friends.

One day in Zimbabwe, Reeve met a twelve-year-old girl who had been blinded by cataracts. All that prevented the girl from regaining her sight was a twenty-dollar surgery that would only take fifteen minutes. Reeve knew there had to be something she could do to help. A few days later, as Reeve and Lolly finished the eighteenth hole on a golf course near their home, they hatched the idea for a charity that would provide cataract surgery for people in need. Through their charity, Eyes4Zimbabwe, they provided sight-restoring surgery to thousands of Zimbabweans.

A few years after Reeve and Lolly started Eyes4Zimbabwe, a woman recruited Reeve to coach her daughter, a professional golfer from Norway. This golfer's name was Cecilie, but everyone called her CC. CC was experiencing a difficult time in her life, with many of her loved ones having recently passed away. Reeve and Lolly listened to her struggles, grieved with her, and gently shared the plan of salvation and the truths of the restored gospel. CC began attending church regularly, at home and on tour, and was baptized soon after. CC also joined Eyes4Zimbabwe and runs the Norwegian chapter.

In Zimbabwe, Reeve met many young men and women who longed to serve missions but could not afford the supplies or the necessary documents and doctor's check-ups. Reeve, CC, and Lolly taught mission preparation classes to these future missionaries and gathered supplies to pack suitcases containing everything new missionaries need. They asked their golf sponsors to donate shipping containers for the suitcases and donations. To their surprise, the sponsors said yes! In 2014, Reeve, Lolly, and CC, along with many other volunteers, were able to provide 1,100 suitcases to departing missionaries from Zimbabwe and Mozambique.

These three women exemplify that when women live their testimonies, they can change the world. As CC said, "We may not change the WHOLE world, but we can change the world for one person."

Chieko Nishimura Okazaki

ONCE UPON A TIME, *there was a little girl in Hawaii watching her mother sweep the floor.* "Chieko," *her mother said.* "I need a kigatsuku *girl.*" *Chieko perked up and quickly fetched the dustpan for her mother. A* kigatsuku *girl is a Japanese term for a girl who sees a need and fills it without being asked. Soon, Chieko's mother didn't need to remind her to be a* kigatsuku *girl—it became part of Chieko's soul.*

Chieko's parents were from Japan and worked on a plantation in Hawaii. They wanted their children to have a better life, so they made slippers with Chieko's brothers' help to save enough money for her to attend college. Her family's sacrifice deeply moved Chieko, and she dedicated her life to education. She met her husband, Ed, while she worked toward her degree in education at the University of Hawaii. When Chieko and Ed moved to Utah in 1951 for Ed's master's degree, Chieko became an elementary school teacher. Anti-Japanese feelings still ran high in the United States in this post-World War II period, and Chieko and Ed faced discrimination at work and in their neighborhood. At times, when members at church were particularly hurtful, they wondered if they should leave the church. But since being baptized at fifteen, Chieko's testimony was strong. She would live the gospel no matter what someone else said.

In 1961, Chieko was called to the Young Women's general board, making her the first person of color to hold a church calling on the general board level. She and Ed also presided over the Japan Okinawa Mission, where they changed many couples' lives through their example of working together as equal partners.

When Chieko was called to the Relief Society general presidency in 1990, she was given a blessing in which she was told that her tongue would be loosed so that she would be able to speak her thoughts and her soul. This blessing gave her the courage to speak about the needs she saw— even though they were topics that hadn't been addressed in the general setting before. She also felt strongly that she needed to address women in their own language, so she practiced her talks in Samoan, Spanish, and Korean until she could deliver the talks without a translator.

Chieko said, "Do you see women of different ages, races or different backgrounds in the Church? Of different educational, marital and professional experiences? Women with children? Women without children? Women of vigorous health and those who are limited by chronic illness or handicaps? Rejoice in the diversity of our sisterhood! It is the diversity of colors in a spectrum that makes a rainbow."

Claire Teriitehau Manea

1931–2016
French Polynesia

ONCE UPON A TIME, *there were two nervous young men standing near the shore on the island of Maupiti, French Polynesia. They were the first Latter-day Saint missionaries to visit the island in more than sixty years. A nurse named Claire paused when she saw them and told her boyfriend, Andre, to invite the two young men to their home for dinner.*

For the next several months, the missionaries taught Claire, Andre, and many other people living on Maupiti. Despite sideways glances from their neighbors who were staunchly devout in their own religion, Claire and Andre were impressed by the gentleness in the missionaries' message. In 1963, members on Maupiti received an invitation from the branch in Huahine, an island one hundred miles away, to attend the dedication of their new chapel. Claire and Andre wanted to attend the celebration together, but since they served as radio and telegram operators, one of them had to stay behind. Andre agreed to man the telegraph station if Claire promised to share what the apostle, Gordon B. Hinckley, taught at the dedication.

The morning of the dedication dawned clear and bright, and the sea was calm. The meeting was beautiful, and the islanders held a large celebration that lasted late into the evening. Claire and the other fifty members from Maupiti dragged themselves away from the party and began the voyage back home.

It was close to dawn when a few passengers on the boat noticed what looked like soap suds floating on the water, an ominous sign that rough waters were ahead. The Maupiti pass is known for being one of the most dangerous sailing routes in the world, and some of the men on board begged the captain not to enter the pass when they saw the roiling water. Before the captain could change course, a massive wave lifted the boat in the air. After a moment when the boat seemed frozen on the crest of the wave, it tumbled into the ocean, flipping three times. Claire was tossed up and down in the waves like a leaf scattered in the water. As the waves threatened to crush her, she prayed with all her heart, "Heavenly Father, save me! If you save me, I will be Thy servant." Moments later, she found herself lying on a reef. She caught her breath and had only a moment to notice her torn clothes, cuts, and bruises before a wave washed her into the sea again. A young man swam to her and threw her a life preserver, which she clung to for hours. In the early morning sunlight, Claire heard the distant sound of a motor. She called out for help, and relief flooded her heart when she saw Andre sailing toward her. He helped Claire onto the boat, and they set about rescuing as many other members as they could find.

Fifteen people were lost in the shipwreck, and President Hinckley came to the island to offer blessings and comfort. He gave a battered Claire a blessing and promised that she would be healed and that God had work for her to do. On July 2, after Claire had recovered for a month, she and Andre were married. The next day they were baptized. Four years later, they were sealed in the Hamilton New Zealand Temple.

Cohn Shoshonitz Zundel

1863–1949
Shoshone Nation

*O*NCE UPON A TIME, *there was a woman named Cohn dancing for her grandchildren. Cohn's beaded moccasins kicked up the dust as she performed a traditional Shoshone dance. As she stomped the earth, her strong legs spoke of the many hours milking her three cows, caring for her thirty-five chickens, and planting and harvesting onions, turnips, beets, potatoes, apples, and watermelon.*

Her arms waved in the air—arms that had held and loved nine babies, of whom only four had lived to adulthood. Her graceful hands were calloused from decades of tanning hides and creating moccasins, gloves, purses, and belts adorned with beautiful beadwork for which the Shoshone are renowned. Her hands were also strong from kneading dough for pies, bread, and cakes—recipes she learned from her Relief Society sisters.

But as Cohn joyfully danced, what her grandchildren saw most of all was her heart. Cohn and her people had experienced terrible heartbreak in her early years. Not only did they mourn for their brothers and sisters who were killed in the Bear River Massacre, but their resources were also slowly eaten up by pioneer settlers and their cattle in the Shoshone's valley. In order to survive, Cohn's tribe had to give up their traditional hunter-gatherer lifestyle for a life of stationary farming.

During this time of transition in Cohn's childhood, her parents taught her about the Creator, who provided all things for them and watched over them. When Cohn was nine years old, a respected tribe leader testified that he saw in a vision that the God of the Latter-day Saints living in the valley was the same Creator they knew and worshiped. When the missionaries were called to preach to Cohn's tribe, more than one hundred people, including Cohn's family, were baptized. The knowledge of a Savior who could heal all heartbreak strengthened her people. They were organized into the Washakie Ward, where they worshiped in their own language. They learned the traditions of the gospel while cherishing and passing on the traditions of their people.

Cohn taught her grandchildren the importance of honoring and remembering their Shoshone heritage and encouraged them to look forward in faith for the Second Coming of the Savior. "Jesus is coming," she said. "While you are waiting, go do your work and learn all you can."

Edith Florence Papworth Weenig Tanner

1899–1984
England

ONCE UPON A TIME, *there was a seventeen-year-old girl named Edith riding through London on the top deck of a double decker bus.*

It was a lovely May Sunday in 1917. Edith was pulled from her enjoyment of the rare London sunshine by a sign that read, "The Mormon Message to the World." When Edith left her home in the English countryside to work in London, her parents warned her about the Mormons. "Stay away from the Mormons," they said. "They are only here to capture young girls and send them to Utah to become polygamist wives."

Sensing an opportunity for adventure, Edith hopped off the bus at the next stop and headed back to the building. Edith was never one to shy away from adventure. When she arrived in London a few years earlier, she began work as a typist in the British War Office. World War I was raging across Europe. Before long, Edith and her friend were recruited to be secret messengers for the British government. They carried messages across the English Channel to the leaders of the British forces in France. If they were caught by enemy soldiers, they were instructed to swallow the messages they carried. Some of Edith's colleagues at the War Office were captured or killed, and Edith herself had a few close calls, even surviving a run-in with an enemy spy!

Now Edith sat in the chapel listening to a new message at a large stake conference. Many people were baptized as part of the conference,

and Edith witnessed several baby blessings, too. When Edith was ten years old, her baby brother, Albert, died. The priest warned Edith's parents that Albert couldn't go to heaven since he hadn't been baptized. After she saw the baby blessings, Edith cautiously approached a missionary and asked about baptism for infants. The missionary explained that little children who died returned to their Heavenly Parents. Edith's heart filled with joy for little Albert. Next, she warily asked the missionary how many wives he had. He laughed and told her he only had one wife and that polygamy had been banned in the Church. Satisfied with his answer, Edith stayed for the rest of the conference, and the Spirit continued to fill her heart. Six months later she was baptized.

Edith's father did not approve of her baptism, and he told her never to come back home. The Christmas Eve after her baptism, she traveled home, arriving at 11:00 p.m. Her father told her she wasn't welcome and sent her to wait at the train station in the wintry night air. Though she missed her family dearly, Edith stayed true to her baptismal covenants. She served a mission in Gravesend, a shipping port at the mouth of the Thames, and lived a life of adventure and faith in England, the United States, and Japan. Through cloud and sunshine and across three continents, the gospel gave Edith courage and faith.

Edith Russell

*O*NCE UPON A TIME, *there was a ten-year-old girl named Edith who grew up on the fringe of wind-swept, rugged moors that inspired the Bronte sisters' classic Gothic novels.*

Perhaps inspired by their legacy, Edith confided in her sometimes-gruff schoolteacher that she wanted to be a great writer. Edith expected him to laugh. Instead, he sent her books to read and entered her in every literary contest available. In Edith's small family cottage, she devoured books and hoped to be immortalized like Shakespeare. Edith's family was not religious, but she was always curious about the church in the valley. She wondered what it would be like to pray, and if God had something for her to do.

When Edith was twenty-three, she worked in a financial office that contributed to England's war effort during World War II. One day a man called Gregory came to Edith's office for training. Sensing something special in Edith's demeanor, he asked her what she would think of a church that had for a principle, "The glory of God is intelligence." Edith was thunderstruck. She asked to know more about his church, The Church of Jesus Christ of Latter-day Saints. Over the next few weeks Gregory taught her the gospel. After overcoming her initial doubts and obstacles (she wasn't so sure about an American prophet who talked like actors in the movies), Edith was baptized on September 26, 1942.

For a full year after her baptism, Edith vowed to put down her pen and her aspirations of authorial fame in order to preach the gospel. Edith focused her time on speaking about Christ at work and in her neighborhood, but something always called her back to writing. She felt her creative talents were gifts from God. "Where else did I get my soul's response to beauty?" she thought.

Edith decided to submit a few pieces to *The Millennial Star*, the Church's magazine in England. One month later, she received a mission call to become an editor for *The Millennial Star*. In the midst of World War II, many of the magazine's editors had been sent to the war front. Edith became the first woman in the *Star's* history to take over the magazine's content and editing responsibilities. It wasn't enough for Edith to merely keep the magazine afloat during the war years. She wanted to make sweeping changes so the magazine would truly benefit the lives of her readers.

Edith lived through countless air raids during her time in London and spent many nights in the mission home's bomb shelter, listening to airplanes whistling overhead. She survived a bomb that landed nearby and shattered every window in the mission home. When the mission home was too damaged to carry on, she moved with the rest of the mission office to Birmingham. Through all this, she wrote articles and edited *The Millennial Star*, sharing her experiences and her testimony with each word of her incredible writing. She never felt alone at her desk. She always felt the Spirit nearby, prompting or restraining.

Edith wrote, "Every *Star* that is born imparts to me the joy of creation. Each one is an adventure. But some day, very soon, my mission will be at an end. When it began, I stood in the darkness and reached for a star. Somewhere, someone laughed at my audacity. When it is finished, I shall stand on a star and reach for the moon. God will not laugh."

Emily States

1977–
United States

ONCE UPON A TIME, there was a girl named Emily who suffered from dreadful migraines. Sometimes, Emily would study for hours to prepare for a test, only to begin the test at school and have it disappear from her vision as pain and nausea from the migraine kicked in. Emily resolved that one day she would become a genetic researcher and find the cause of her terrible headaches.

As Emily followed her passion for science and genetic research, some people were unkind to her. They told her that she couldn't be a woman of faith and pursue a career in molecular biology and genetics. These comments were hurtful, but Emily knew that God had sent her on this path. She knew her talents and opportunities came from her Heavenly Parents.

Emily earned a doctorate degree in genetics from Harvard Medical School and completed a postdoctoral fellowship at the University of San Francisco Medical School. She then became a professor at Brigham Young University and started two projects. In one project she studied the genetic causes of migraines, and in the other she studied causes of facial birth defects. Emily made important discoveries in how sleep patterns affect migraines. She also made exciting discoveries about how disruptions in ion channels can cause facial defects in babies. Scientists knew ion channels regulated electricity in the brain and muscles, but Emily discovered that ion channels also sent signals to babies growing in the womb that tell each cell what to become. Emily said discovering something no one else knows as a scientist is "like being on a mountaintop—it's so exciting. There's almost nothing else like it in the world."

Sometimes, people ask Emily about the conflicts between religion and science, and she says simply that they are complementary approaches to finding the truth. When science and religion seem to conflict, Emily prays and studies. Through the Spirit, she discerns what is true or how the two concepts can work together. She believes everything good is from God and that all truth leads to Him.

Emma Hale Smith

ONCE UPON A TIME, there was a schoolteacher named Emma who had lovely penmanship and a brave heart. Emma was educated, wealthy, beautiful, and clever. Her parents expected her to marry a man from their town—a man with money and good standing.

Emma's life changed when she met a young man named Joseph Smith. He was uneducated and did not come from a wealthy family. But Emma saw that Joseph had integrity and was a hardworking, intelligent man. She wanted to marry him more than any man she had ever met. Against her parents' wishes, she eloped with Joseph and embarked on a journey that would require more of her heart than she could have ever imagined.

Emma believed in the restored gospel. Her testimony and love for Joseph gave her the courage to leave everything she had known and dedicate her life to the kingdom of God. Her beautiful, careful penmanship bolstered the building of the Church on countless occasions. Emma was the first scribe for Joseph while he translated the Book of Mormon. She also served as his tutor, helping him with pronunciation and historical background to understand the stories he translated. This experience solidified her testimony of the Book of Mormon and of her husband's prophetic calling.

Later in their marriage, Joseph received revelation that Emma was to compile a hymnbook for the Church. In Emma's time, male clergy always compiled hymnals, but with the help of several members of the Church, she compiled a beautiful collection of hymns.

Man times Joseph had to go into hiding or was imprisoned for crimes he did not commit. Emma's beautiful writing again brought comfort to Joseph as she wrote uplifting and encouraging letters to her husband. "Again, she is here," Joseph reflected, "even in the seventh trouble, undaunted, firm and unwavering, unchangeable, affectionate Emma!"

Emma faced countless sorrows throughout her life, including the deaths of six children and the martyrdom of her husband. Before Joseph left for Carthage Jail, Emma asked for a blessing. Joseph asked her to write the blessing she desired. Her faith again shone through her writing as she expressed her desire for "the Spirit of God to know and understand [herself]" and "that whatever be [her] lot through life, [she] may be enabled to acknowledge the hand of God in all things."

Her mother-in-law, Lucy, wrote: "I have never seen a woman in my life, who would endure every species of fatigue and hardship, from month to month and from year to year, with that unflinching courage, zeal, and patience, which she has ever done."

23

Esohe Frances Ikponmwen

1954–
Nigeria

ONCE UPON A TIME, there was a woman named Esohe taking an oath of office as Chief Judge of Edo State in Nigeria. The governor of Edo State told her, "Your wealth of experience as a judge and your ability to discharge your duty without fear or favor is enough signal that you are ready and qualified to lead our state judiciary." Esohe (now Honorable Justice Esohe Frances Ikponmwen) smiled to herself, remembering how far she had come.

More than forty years earlier, Esohe had been a young law student at the University of Nigeria, pregnant with her first child. She and her friend, who was also pregnant, worried that by becoming lawyers they would be "bigger than their husbands," who were working as civil servants. They worried that this would hurt their marriages, so they sought counsel from their faculty adviser about changing their course of study. He smiled kindly at them and told them to take a seat. "There are hundreds of people clamoring for a law degree," he told them. "You have been chosen by the university. Be grateful and brave. Continue your studies and they will lead you to countless opportunities." Esohe and her friend decided to stay.

After graduating from university, Esohe worked in the office of the attorney general. It was her first job as a lawyer, and she worried she didn't have the gift of advocacy. She thought she wouldn't be able to speak well in court because she was shy and soft-spoken. When she received her first case, a simple bill matter in front of the high court, she was terrified. She sought advice from the other women who had been practicing law longer than she had. She even asked one fellow lawyer to accompany her to the court so she wasn't alone. Because of her preparation, she performed brilliantly. From that day on, she knew she could succeed as a lawyer.

Throughout Esohe's journey, women mentored her and bolstered her confidence both professionally and spiritually. When Esohe began investigating the Church, she sought advice from another lawyer, Belinda Kalu. She and Belinda examined the Church's doctrines and Esohe's questions from the perspective of their legal training. Esohe gained comfort and confidence through her conversations with Belinda, and she gained confirmation from the Spirit as she prayed about the Book of Mormon. On the day she was baptized, she knew she was in the right place, and that feeling never left her.

Far from the nervous and soft-spoken young woman she had been, Honorable Justice Ikponmwen was now revered for her integrity and fearlessness in court. After taking her oath of office, a group of reporters asked about her attitude toward her work. She quoted King Benjamin: "When ye are in the service of your fellow beings, ye are only in the service of your God" (Mosiah 2:17).

Florence Chukwurah

1946–
Nigeria

ONCE UPON A TIME, *there was a girl named Florence selling bitterleaf at a market in Onitsha, Nigeria, while the rest of her classmates enjoyed a holiday from school. Florence's mother and father worked hard to provide food and a home for her family, but if Florence wanted an education, she had to earn the money herself.*

When Florence was eleven years old, she dreamed of escaping poverty. She made four resolutions to reach her goal:

1. Seek God earnestly.
2. Be obedient to parents and elders.
3. Take schoolwork seriously.
4. Work hard with my hands.

Florence was no stranger to working hard. She often hauled water from public taps and streams to her family home, and she fetched firewood from the countryside and chopped it into cooking fuel. She was dedicated to her schoolwork and spent every holiday selling vegetables at the market.

One day, on her way home from the market, Florence passed the bustling hospital. She noticed the nurses in their bright white nursing caps. She imagined herself wearing the crisp uniform and cap, nursing patients back to health. When she learned that the government would help her pay for nursing school, her course was set. At sixteen years old, Florence began nursing school and worked toward becoming a midwife. The year she graduated from her training at Queen Elizabeth Hospital, she was given the Florence Nightingale Award for best nurse of the year!

Many years later, Florence and her husband, Christopher, were called to preside over the Ghana Accra Mission. Florence helped reduce sickness among the missionaries with the skills she learned in her years of nursing. When she met young people whose poverty made them timid, she felt prompted to tell them about her life. As Florence shared her life story, their eyes lit up with hope and potential. "You are the future of Africa," she told them. "Appreciate what you have, but also work hard to improve on it, using creativity and imagination."

Gladys Knight

1944–
United States

ONCE UPON A TIME, there was a little girl named Gladys who would one day be known as the Empress of Soul. Little Gladys sang gospel songs crowded around a beat-up piano with her family. Gladys's mother always told her that music was a gift from God to be freely shared. Gladys's parents loved music, and they encouraged her to sing in front of the Mount Mariah Baptist Church in Atlanta, Georgia, when she was only four years old.

Gladys's music career began in earnest when she was a teenager. She sang in a group called Gladys Knight and the Pips with her brothers and cousins, and they recorded many chart-topping hits and won two Grammy awards. Sometimes Gladys wanted to leave musical performance to enjoy a normal life, but she felt that God had given her the gift of music, and she was determined to continue on the path He laid out for her. She found great success in her music career, winning seven Grammy awards and performing all over the world.

Shortly after Gladys was inducted into the Rock and Roll Hall of Fame, she felt a desire to be more spiritual. She had always treasured her faith in God, and she now wanted to know more about His plan. Two of her children had already been baptized into The Church of Jesus Christ of Latter-day Saints, and they invited her to listen to the missionaries. To Gladys's delight, the missionaries answered her questions and helped her find the path to grow closer to the Savior. She was baptized by her son in 1997.

Gladys faced challenges in her early years of Church membership. She received questions and criticism for joining the Church because of its history of excluding Black people from priesthood ordinations and temple blessings. Gladys responded that the more the members immersed themselves in the gospel, the less they judged others on the way they looked. "It's time for people of color to come to His church," she said. "It's just our time."

The other challenge Gladys faced was adapting to the more solemn and reserved form of worship that was so different from the vibrant and energetic meetings of her youth. She decided to start a choir called Saints Unified Voices that would bring new energy and cultural diversity to traditional hymns. The goals of the choir were to spread the message of the restored gospel and help members embrace the cultural diversity of the worldwide membership of the Church. Wherever the choir performed, hundreds of missionary referrals followed.

Whenever Gladys performs, whether with the Saints Unified Voiced Choir or on her own, she prays that the audience will be able to see the light of the gospel shining through her performance and that they will know that they are children of God. "I'm using what the Lord gave me," she said. "I'm not perfect, but I'm striving to be what He wants me to be."

GLADYS NANG'ONI
NASSIUMA SITATI

Gladys Nang'oni Nassiuma Sitati

1952–
Kenya

*O*NCE UPON A TIME, *there was a little girl in Kenya who was a very quick learner. Her father, an English and math teacher who cared deeply about the education of his ten children, took Gladys under his wing and personally tutored her. He took her to school with him and made sure she was a diligent enough student to be accepted at a good boarding school..*

As Gladys continued her schooling, she taught her younger siblings and helped with their schoolwork. At Nairobi University, where she was studying education, she met a man named Joseph. As they began a relationship, Gladys and Joseph were shocked to learn they were from the same town. Shock turned to suspicion that they might be related. Luckily, there was no relation, and they married three years later when Gladys finished her degree in education.

In the next seven years, the Sitatis had five children, and Gladys taught at the schools her siblings attended and at a teaching college. In 1983, after the birth of her fifth child, she became an administrator in the Ministry of Education. Two years later, an American Latter-day Saint couple living in Nairobi met the Sitatis at a mutual friend's house and invited them to church. Gladys and her family were baptized a year later and began frequent family councils.

After seven years with the Ministry of Education, Gladys felt prompted to make a change. She and

Joseph counseled together, and with the support of the Spirit, they decided that Gladys would quit her job and work at home with the children.

Many years later, Joseph and Gladys were called to preside over the Nigeria Uyo Mission. Although they served in an English-speaking country, Gladys noticed that many missionaries struggled with English. Using the skills she had gained in seven years as a professional educator and forty years teaching her children, she created a curriculum for the struggling missionaries. She taught thirty-minute lessons at every zone conference, assigning homework and providing feedback on the last conference's homework until the missionaries were fluent in English.

Gladys's Heavenly Parents blessed her with unique teaching talents that blessed her children and countless others as she served alongside her husband and followed the voice of the Spirit.

Haju Julloh

UNKNOWN

Sierra Leone

*O*NCE UPON A TIME, in Sierra Leone, a deadly disease called the Ebola virus swept across the land. The first case was reported in the spring of 2014, and in the months after, thousands of people were infected with the terrible plague and died. In July of that year, government troops entered areas where the disease was most vicious and enforced quarantines to try to contain the spread of the virus. In the midst of the disease and quarantines, many people lost their jobs and struggled to find food and water for their families.

Amid these trials, a woman named Haju began learning about the Church. The peace of the gospel gave her hope as she worked each day as a nurse treating Ebola patients. Haju spent each day breathing hot, humid air behind a face mask and plastic face shield, placing IVs in infected patients and offering comfort where she could. At the end of each exhausting shift, she peeled off her protective gown and placed it with other contaminated gowns and linens to be washed by the hospital. When she wasn't working, Haju learned from the missionaries, and she decided to be baptized.

One day in August, shortly after her baptism, Haju's protective gown wasn't thoroughly cleaned. She pulled it on and worked her shift as she always did, but a few days later she woke with a fever and a terrible pain in her head. Haju hoped desperately that she was only overtired from her long hours of work or that she had caught a cold, but her Ebola test came back with the dreaded positive. Haju began quarantining in her home. Many of her nursing colleagues had succumbed to the disease, and Haju grappled with the possibility that the same might happen to her. Haju decided to spend her time in quarantine concentrat-

ing on her Book of Mormon studies. She read the stories of Alma the Younger being brought out of a three-day fever and of Ammon lifting King Lamoni up from what his people thought was certain death. As she read about miracles that happened to ordinary people like her in the scriptures, she began to nurture a small seed of hope that she might receive her own miracle.

After a few weeks, Haju's fever disappeared, along with her headache and all other symptoms of the disease. Hardly daring to believe that she was cured, Haju was tested again for the virus. This time the test was negative! The health department asked her to quarantine for another week before being tested again. It was agonizing to wait, but she found comfort in the Book of Mormon. After a week passed, she was tested again. Negative! Haju's heart overflowed with gratitude at her miraculous recovery. She was finally able to leave her house and return to church, where her friends welcomed her back with joy. Haju also quickly returned to work and continued to treat Ebola patients with both hope and empathy and with the knowledge that God had heard her prayers and given her a miracle.

Irma de McKenna

ONCE UPON A TIME, there was a woman named Irma who was buoyant with joy. She practically bounced down the road in Quilpué, Chile, with her baby in her arms. Irma, a schoolteacher, had recently been baptized. Her husband and two teenage children had not joined her when she decided to be baptized, but she felt like a magic light inside her allowed her to bear all her tests with happiness. Irma was on her way to her mother's house and was brimming with excitement at the chance to tell her more about the gospel.

When Irma began to explain the Restoration to her mother, her other family members butted in, saying Joseph Smith was a false prophet. They refused to read the pamphlets the missionaries had given Irma, and they laughed when she tried to offer them a Book of Mormon.

As Irma trudged home, the bounce had gone from her step, and the light was gone from her eyes. The road was dark and misty, but it couldn't compare to the darkness in Irma's heart. She entered her house crying, with her baby in her arms. Irma tried to hide the pain in her soul as she served dinner to her husband and older children. Irma's husband didn't support her conversion and became angry when he saw her pray, so Irma waited until he fell asleep to quietly sit up and pray. Irma poured her sorrow out in prayer. She felt alone and ashamed that she hadn't known enough about the gospel to defend it against her family's slanders. She promised to study the scriptures harder and pleaded for help to find the light that had illuminated her soul after her baptism.

Irma wasn't sure how long she was there, or if she had fallen asleep, but in the darkness of her room she saw a vision of a hand gently placed upon her head. The hand was luminous, perfect, and beautiful. She felt all the sadness leave her heart as it was replaced with peace and joy. Irma knew she wasn't alone, and she knew that no matter what trials she faced, the Lord knew her and would be there to comfort and lift her. After five years of Irma keeping her promise to study the scriptures and defend her faith, Irma's mother was baptized.

Irma and her mother both faced many trials, but Irma always carried with her the feeling of love and peace from her vision on that dark night that filled her with light.

Juana Bautista Zúñiga

1882–1984
Mexico

ONCE UPON A TIME, there was a little girl named Juana who was born in the shadow of a holy mountain in Mexico called Popocatépetl. From the time she was very young, Juana was a bright spot in her family and community. Her mother owned a store, a meat market, and a bakery, and her father owned a lumberyard. When Juana was fourteen, she followed in her parents' entrepreneurial footsteps and started a thriving business selling wooden crates and containers fifty miles away in Mexico City.

Around this time, the missionaries started visiting Juana's brother, Margarito. Juana joined the lessons and listened intently to the message. Her face glowed with joy as she felt the Spirit testify that the Book of Mormon was true. After a few months, she and Margarito were baptized.

One Sunday when Juana was seventeen, the mission president asked if anyone in Sunday School would like to share an insight about a verse from the scriptures. Juana's hand shot in the air, and her eyes sparkled as she shared her testimony of the Book of Mormon. Juana was so exhilarated by the experience that she carefully studied her scriptures each week to be able to share her insights every Sunday. Soon the Sunday School room was full to bursting with her friends and neighbors who came to hear her speak.

Juana married her husband, José, another pioneering member of the Church in Mexico, when she was twenty-one. Early in their marriage, José lost his job. Juana and José prayed for guidance to support their growing family, and Juana felt inspired to make and sell embroidered scarves and handkerchiefs. At first, the townspeople said they didn't have the money for her goods, but when they saw that Juana had already embroidered their names or initials on the items, they changed their minds. Juana and her family had plenty to eat because of her business savvy.

Juana and José lived in many towns in Mexico and the United States. Wherever they went, they shared their enterprising spirits and glowing testimonies with anyone who would listen. They were instrumental in the establishment of the local Mexican Mission in Salt Lake City, and Juana started several businesses, including a grocery store, *J. Zúñiga, Abarrotes y Panadería*, all while raising eight children. What her grandchildren remembered best about Juana was her shining, happy face each time she bore her testimony and the tears that streamed down her wrinkled cheeks each time she prayed for them. In her hundred years of life, she built a legacy of industry, love, and light.

Julia Mavimbela

1917–2000
South Africa

ONCE UPON A TIME, there was a woman named Julia in Soweto, South Africa, gently placing a seed in a hole with weathered hands. Julia studied the group of children surrounding her and said, "Let us dig the soil of bitterness, throw in a seed of love, and see what fruits it can give us." Julia's beautiful garden, once a hardened, rodent infested plot, was now a haven for children after the Soweto Uprising of 1976.

The Soweto Uprising had started with a group of high schoolers peacefully protesting apartheid, a system in South Africa that separated people based on their race and skin color. The protest had turned violent, and many young people had been killed by police sent to quell the riots. School had been canceled, and many parents had lost their jobs, so the children came to the garden to grow food for their families, continue their studies, and find refuge from the chaos outside. Julia created the garden because she had recognized bitterness and hate in the youth that she had once felt in her own heart, and she knew she needed to help.

Nearly twenty years earlier, Julia's husband, John, had been killed in a car accident, leaving her a widow and mother of six children. John had been active in a political group that opposed apartheid, and he had been a successful businessman. The accident seemed suspicious, but Julia was never able to press charges and find justice. Julia's grief and anger plagued her until she remembered how the Savior forgave the soldiers who crucified Him. She wanted to help the youth find peace, too. Using her background as an educator—she was the first black female prin-

cipal in her province—she taught both English and life lessons in her gardens as she taught the youth to grow food, flowers, and trees. She helped them find common ground and feel responsible for the beauty in their town.

While Julia served the youth in her ward and her community in Soweto, she also worked for the betterment of women and children in all of South Africa. She helped found Women for Peace, a group that advocates for equal rights and morality in government, and she established more than 780 branches of an organization called Women of African Independent Churches, whose mission is to eliminate illiteracy among black women.

Julia said in a speech at the 1975 regional conference of the National Council of African Women, "I give thanks to God that he has made me a woman. I give thanks to my Creator that he has made me black, that he has fashioned me as I am with hands, heart, head to serve my people. It can, it should be a glorious thing to be a woman."

Laura Asioli

1983–
Italy

ONCE UPON A TIME, there was a little girl named Laura who knew exactly what she wanted to be when she grew up. Laura had recently been baptized with her mother. Laura loved to hear scriptures that spoke of Jesus as her advocate with the Father.

When she learned about lawyers and their role as advocates for their clients, Laura knew she would become a lawyer. She thrilled at the idea of helping others to obtain justice. When she began law school many years later, she felt the Spirit confirm to her that she was on the right path. Day by day, her conviction that divinity and justice were intertwined grew stronger.

Laura graduated from law school and landed a coveted two-year training experience. All that was left to do was sit for her exams, and she would be on her way to the career of her dreams. When Laura got the exam results, she was shocked. She had failed! When she appealed the result, the professor told her that there had been mistakes in the grading of her test, but there was nothing he could do. She would have to take the exam again. Laura was heartbroken. She had studied diligently and was living the gospel. Why had this happened to her?

Laura was able to keep her training experience position, but she had to wait until she retook the exam six months later. For those six months she worked in a temporary position at a compliance law firm. Years later, after her husband lost his job in an economic downturn, Laura had a chance meeting with her old boss. She offered Laura's husband a job, and a little while later, she offered Laura a job with the flexibility to enjoy a career she loved as well as motherhood with her two small children.

Laura realized that much of the good that came to her family's life during those years came because of her failed exam. She remembered her patriarchal blessing, which promised her that if she would put her family first, Heavenly Father would open doors in her career and she would always be able to balance both responsibilities. Laura knew that God would help her as she strived to be like Christ in her work as a lawyer and as a mother.

Lucille Bankhead

1902–1994
United States

ONCE UPON A TIME, there was a young woman named Lucille picking tiny red currant berries from a bush on her family's farm. In summers past, she snuck berries as she picked, enjoying the sweet, tangy juice, but after picking them every summer for as long as she could remember, she could barely look at a currant berry, let alone eat one.

Lucille grew up on a family farm in a mostly Black community near Salt Lake City, Utah. Every Sunday, Lucille attended church, even though her mother and father often stayed home. She loved to attend Sunday School and learn from spiritual teachers who helped her understand the Bible and the Book of Mormon. While Lucille felt warmth and comfort from attending church, she also felt confused and hurt by the Church's policy that prohibited Black members from receiving the priesthood or attending the temple. It felt wrong to Lucille, so she prayed and studied the scriptures to understand. When she read that "God is no respecter of persons" she knew that she was equal in God's eyes and that one day she would be able to enter the temple. In 1978, after the ban was lifted, Lucille entered the temple for her own endowment and later served as proxy for her ancestors who hadn't been able to enter the temple.

Lucille's confidence in God's love for her gave her the courage to speak up when people tried to treat her differently for the color of her skin. On one occasion, she was asked to give a speech for the Daughters of Utah Pioneers, where she had served as secretary for four years. The doorman opened the door for Lucille's friends, but before she could enter the room, the doorman closed the door on Lucille and told her she had to go through the kitchen entrance. Lucille stood her ground and refused to go through a different entrance until the doorman sheepishly opened the door for her. At every meeting after that, the doorman didn't hesitate to open the door wide for Lucille.

In 1939, a Utah senator began a campaign that would force Black Salt Lake City residents to move into a segregated area to be known as the "black district." At Lucille's art and craft club, she and the other women spoke about how ridiculous the campaign was. Many of the women had lived in their homes with their families for generations, and they refused to be forced off of their land. Lucille and a few of the women from the club packed a lunch, loaded up their horse and wagon, and rode to the Utah legislature. They sat in the legislature all day, and even though Lucille had her infant son with her, she was the boldest in demanding to be heard. Because of the efforts of Lucille and her friends, the campaign didn't receive enough votes and Lucille and her neighbors kept their land.

Lucille said, "If I don't like what you're doing, I think I'm right, I'm going to open my mouth. I'm going to talk about it. And somebody's going to hear. And if they don't like it, why that's just too bad. . . . I'm a woman, don't make no difference what color my skin is. I bleed just like you do. And I'm going to say what I want to say."

Kelsey Nixon

1987–
United States

*O*NCE UPON A TIME, there was a girl named Kelsey in front of a camera filming her very first cooking show. Kelsey's warmest childhood memories centered on tables full of delicious food surrounded by beloved family members and friends.

As Kelsey grew up, she found she had a passion for setting and achieving lofty goals. When she came across an application for a competitive internship in New York City at a large TV company, she didn't hesitate. She had just finished the first year of her degree in broadcast journalism, and the internship solidified her dream to work in food TV.

In the fall after her internship, Kelsey approached her professor about creating and hosting a college cooking show. "Film a pilot and we'll see," he said. Kelsey wrote a six-episode pilot season, found a local cooking store that would allow her to film in their showroom, and bribed friends with homemade treats to help her film and produce the episodes. After seeing her pilot, Kelsey's professor arranged university support for her show, *Kelsey's Kitchen*, which aired more than 100 episodes in two years!

As Kelsey finished her culinary school training, she auditioned for *Food Network Star*. Her genuine, optimistic personality won audiences over,

and while she finished the show in fourth place, she was voted fan favorite. One of the professionals she befriended on the show, a famous chef named Bobby Flay, offered to produce her cooking show, *Kelsey's Essentials*, on the Cooking Channel.

During the five seasons of filming for *Kelsey's Essentials*, Kelsey and her husband experienced both the joy of adding a baby boy to their family and the sorrow of losing their second son. Though they knew they would be reunited with their son someday, their grief was like a gray cloud that hung around them. The clouds began to break and allow healing to pour in as Kelsey found her passion again for cooking and sharing meals as a family. A few years later, Kelsey and her husband added a miracle baby to their family, and Kelsey continued to juggle motherhood and her career. "It's important to be kind to yourself," she said. "If you don't fit the 'mold' it's okay!"

Lidia Zakrewski

1924–2011
Poland

ONCE UPON A TIME, there was a seventeen-year-old girl named Lidia who loved to play the piano and delivered messages for the Polish Resistance amid raining gunfire and bombs. When the Nazis occupied Poland in World War II, they forbade Poles from pursuing higher education and banned the works of Polish composers, writers, and artists. Like many of her countrymen, Lidia felt great pride in her heritage. She determined to finish her education and join the resistance.

Lidia studied medicine at the underground University of Warsaw and music at the underground Conservatory of Music, where professors taught in abandoned factories and buildings under penalty of death.

One day, while Lidia carried messages for the Polish Resistance during the sixty-three-day Warsaw Uprising, she stumbled upon a piano blocking a hole in the wall of a bombed-out school. Gazing at the piano, Lidia felt a mixture of weariness for the fighting and bloodshed she had witnessed and love for her country.

Lidia placed her hands on the keys of the miraculously intact piano and played "Revolutionary Etude" by Poland's beloved composer, Chopin. As Lidia's fingers flew across the keys, the sharp sounds of bullets pummeling the back of the piano interrupted her playing. Realizing that the thick wood of the piano protected her, Lidia continued to play the beautiful song. Halfway through the Etude, the sound of bullets quieted. As the final notes faded, she heard the soldiers clapping and shouting, "Bravo!" For a short moment, the power of music had paused the fighting.

Lidia was awarded with a cross for bravery for her efforts in the Polish Resistance. After the war, she immigrated to the United States with her husband and three little sons, where she earned her master's degree and PhD in literature. In 1974, thirty years after the Warsaw Uprising, her youngest son invited her to his baptism into The Church of Jesus Christ of Latter-day Saints. At his baptism, Lidia felt a new kind of music in her soul, and she was soon baptized, too. Lidia then became a messenger for Christ, translating Church materials into Polish for her friends, serving three missions, and submitting more than 250,000 names of her Polish family members to the temple.

Liriel Domiciano

1981–
Brazil

ONCE UPON A TIME, there was a little girl who lived in Brazil and loved to sing. Liriel's parents recognized her musical talents but couldn't afford singing lessons. That didn't stop little Liriel from developing her voice. For hours at a time, she listened to classical music, imitating the beautiful voices she heard. By age five, Liriel sang difficult classical arias on her own.

Liriel's parents taught her to have faith in God. Sometimes she felt frustrated that she couldn't take music lessons, and she worried that her dream of becoming a lyric soprano would never come true. In these moments, she heard the Spirit whisper in her mind, "Be calm. It isn't your time yet. God will try you, but all these things are for your growth."

A few years later, as Liriel filled out a seamstress application at a bridal fair, she heard another young woman auditioning to be a wedding singer. She left her seamstress application unfinished and seized the opportunity to share her talent. As she sang the final notes of her audition song— complicated aria by Puccini—the judges were speechless. Within two days, Liriel had ten job offers! Excited by Liriel's success, her friends encouraged her to audition for a popular Brazilian TV talent show called *The Raul Gil Amateur Show*. When Liriel passed the auditions, her dreams were finally in reach! However, Liriel was crestfallen when the producers forbade her from talking about her religion on the show. She was committed to keeping her baptismal promise to stand as a witness of Christ. Before her first performance on TV, Liriel prayed in her dressing room to know how to share her beliefs. She looked up and saw her Young Women medallion hanging from her mirror. Liriel smiled and thanked God for her answer. The medallion represented her commitment to Jesus Christ, so she wore it proudly for every performance. Liriel's thousands of hours of practice and faith in God's timing paid off when she and her partner won the talent show, and their first album became the second highest classical bestseller in Brazilian history.

In 2004, three years after the release of her first bestselling album, Liriel stood in front of more than 20,000 people in the Conference Center and sang with the Tabernacle Choir at Temple Square. It was the first time a soloist had performed in general conference in more than seventy years. She said, "I continue to pray to my Father in Heaven that He can help and teach me to sing with the Spirit like the choir, so that perhaps, I, too, can help his children."

Lucy Mack Smith

1775–1856
United States

ONCE UPON A TIME, *on a cold muddy road in New York, Lucy prepared for another day's journey with her eight children. Her teenage son, Alvin, raced to her side, out of breath. He told her that Mr. Howard, who was supposed to drive their wagon to their new home in Palmyra, had thrown their belongings into the street!*

Mr. Howard planned to steal the wagon and abandon them. Bold, unconquerable Lucy marched into the bar where Mr. Howard sat drunk and told him, "I have no use for you, I shall take charge of the team myself."

Lucy took her belongings and her family, including a toddler, an infant, and eleven-year-old Joseph Jr., who still struggled to walk after his grueling leg surgery four years earlier, and made the one-hundred-mile trip over snowy and muddy roads to Palmyra, where her husband was waiting. When she saw the joy of her family in being reunited with their father, she knew the journey had been worth it.

Many years later, her son Joseph, now the prophet, received revelation that the Saints should move to Ohio. Lucy was elected to be the leader of a traveling company of eighty Saints.

When the company's boat became stranded in an icy river, many of the Saints who had not packed enough food for the delay worried they wouldn't reach Ohio. Eventually the Saints' anxiety boiled over and some started shouting and arguing. Lucy marched up to the group with fire in her eyes and told the group to be faithful, and that if they would pray together, they would be delivered. At that moment, the crowd heard a sound like a thunderclap and the ice broke! The ship barely scraped through the narrow gap in the ice before it closed again for three more weeks.

Lucy, or Mother Smith, as the Saints lovingly called her, spent her life helping souls through the muddy roads and icy obstacles of their lives to find the truthfulness of the gospel. She truly lived by her own counsel: "We must cherish one another, comfort one another, and gain instruction that we may all sit down in heaven together."

Maria teresa toro Valenzuela

1945–
Chile

ONCE UPON A TIME, there was a girl named Maria who grew up in a land bathed by the sea on the east and protected by the mighty Andes mountain range on the west. Maria was born 135 years after Chile gained their independence, and she loved celebrating Chile's Independence Day every September 11 with her close-knit family. She loved the food, music, and dancing. Most of all, Maria loved the traditional dresses of La Cueca, a traditional dance in Chile. The bright flowery fabrics flowed and swayed as the men and women waved their handkerchiefs and stepped across the dance floor.

Maria's father was a military dentist, and her mother was a nurse. They expected Maria to become a nurse like her mother, but Maria loved sewing more than anything. She had been making doll costumes for her neighbors since she was a little girl. Maria's parents relented, and she attended a seamstress school for women. After she graduated, she began her career as a dressmaker, specializing in traditional Chilean attire.

When Maria was a young mother, she and her husband, Alfonso, searched for a church where they felt they belonged. One day, they decided to try a meeting at The Church of Jesus Christ of Latter-day Saints. As they walked through the door, Alfonso whispered to Maria, "It seems they are very rich people—they are all so well dressed and clean." Alfonso and Maria sat in the congregation nervously, but as they listened to the messages and testimonies, their worries melted away. Alfonso and Maria determined that if they saw the missionaries on the street, they would invite them to teach their family. The following Tuesday, the missionaries knocked on Maria and Alfonso's door. Maria was shocked and asked who had sent the two young men, but she realized the Lord had sent them. Maria and Alfonso and their daughters were baptized a short time later.

With her baptism, Maria found a new focus and foundation. As she worked with her dressmaking clients, she discovered a growing ability to listen with love and treat even the most difficult clients with kindness and patience. Each day, before she picked up her scissors and fabric, she prayed for inspiration and guidance. Her divine role as a creator found an outlet in the beautiful dresses she made for each customer.

Mary Elizabeth Rollins

1818–1913
United States

ONCE UPON A TIME, there was a girl named Mary who woke up before the sun rose to read a book. When she was twelve, three missionaries came to her town and taught about a prophet named Joseph Smith and a record called the Book of Mormon. Mary's neighbor, Brother Morley, received a copy of the newly printed book—the only one in the whole county! Mary longed to read it.

One night, Mary walked by herself to his farm to ask if she could borrow the book. Brother Morley was hesitant to give it to her. He hadn't yet had a chance to read it himself. However, seeing her earnestness, Brother Morley said, "If you bring the book back before breakfast tomorrow, you can take it."

Mary could hardly contain her excitement. She and her family took turns reading from the Book of Mormon until late that night, and Mary woke up before anyone else the next day to continue reading the wonderful book.

She returned the book to Brother Morley before breakfast, as promised. He joked with her about how she couldn't have read very far or remembered anything in such a short time. She excitedly recited the first verse of the book for him and told the story of Nephi and his family that she had read the night before. He stared at her for a moment then said, "Take this book home and finish it. I can wait." Mary was the first person in Kirtland to finish the Book of Mormon.

When Mary was fifteen and living in Independence, Missouri, an angry mob attacked their town. The mob destroyed the printing press where Joseph Smith's revelations were being printed and threw many printed sheets out a window to be burned. Realizing that these sheets contained revelation from the prophet, Mary and her thirteen-year-old sister, Caroline, ran to the building and gathered as many pages as they could carry. As they ran away, members of the mob saw them and chased them. Mary and Caroline raced into a corn field and laid on top of the papers to hide them. The sisters shivered with fear as the mob pushed through the corn nearby, and they prayed that God would protect them. Eventually the mob gave up looking for them, and Mary and her sister were able to get the papers to safety. These papers would later become part of the Doctrine and Covenants.

Mary's knowledge of the importance and truth of the scriptures helped her endure persecution and the loss of two children. She said many years later, "The powers of darkness will come to you, but put your trust in your Heavenly Father; let Him be your guide and support, for He is the everlasting light."

Mary Isabella Hales Horne

1818–1905
United States

ONCE UPON A TIME, *a fourteen-year-old girl from England prepared to leave for Tasmania with her family. Her name was Mary Isabella Hales Horne, but her friends called her Isabella. One day, her father received a brochure about the beauty and promise of Toronto, Canada, and they immediately changed their plans. Without this change, Isabella may not have become the hero she was meant to be.*

In Toronto, she and her husband found the Church and were baptized. Soon after, they gathered with the Saints in Missouri and journeyed to the Salt Lake Valley by wagon.

When Isabella was a new member of the Church, she embraced the spiritual gift of divine healing. She combined that power with medical knowledge and instituted a nurses training program. Part of her training program was implemented by the Relief Society in Salt Lake, and she served on the Deseret Hospital Board of Directors for twelve years.

Isabella served in many leadership positions during her life. She served as the president of the Relief Society of the Salt Lake Stake of Zion for twenty-six years! According to her friend Emmeline, Isabella was "a woman of great force of character and wonderful ability, such a one as might stand at the head of a great institution and carry it on successfully." Although it may sound like leadership came naturally to Isabella, she was, by nature, very timid. Through her dedication and faith, she became a powerful leader.

Isabella was also a skilled and thoughtful speaker and a major player in the women's suffrage movement in Utah. She was one of few chosen to represent Latter-day Saint Women at the World's Congress of Representative Women at the Chicago World's Fair of 1893.

Her friend and fellow suffragette, Emmeline B. Wells, said of Isabella, "Sister Horne can appropriately be called a stalwart, a champion for the rights of her own sex, and indeed for all mankind. . . . She . . . spoke with great earnestness and was wise in her utterances, prophetic in nature, familiar with the scriptures, and handled her subjects well. Like others of her time, she was undoubtedly a woman of destiny."

Maud May Babcock

1867–1954
United States

*O*NCE UPON A TIME, *there was a petite girl named Maud who had a voice no one could ignore. At seventeen years old, Maud took a two-year course at the Philadelphia School of Oratory and graduated with honors. Part of her oratory education included physical exercise meant to strengthen the lungs. For Maud, who had traded hours of running through the meadows with her friends for hours in her father's library, her new physical fitness was a wonder. She felt new energy and liveliness she had never known, and vowed to share her blooming passion for educating the whole person—body and mind.*

Five years later, Maud taught courses at the Harvard University School of Physical Education while taking classes in rhetoric and oratory. One of her students was named Susa Young Gates, a member of The Church of Jesus Christ of Latter-day Saints from Salt Lake City. Susa convinced Maud to gp to Utah and teach at the University of Utah. Maud only intended to visit Utah for four months but ended up staying on the University of Utah faculty for forty-six years. She found dear friends, Susa among them, who introduced her to the gospel, and it wasn't long before she was baptized.

Maud was the first female chair of a department at the University of Utah and founded the Department of Physical Education and the Department of Speech. She taught class each day impeccably dressed and graded her students' papers in vibrant purple ink. She staged the first play ever produced by a university: a play based on Greek mythology with one hundred of her female students. Maud also loved basketball and introduced the sport to the university, coaching the women's team until 190—a full decade before the men's basketball team would be established. Maud found spiritual lessons all around her. She loved to admire God's creations on vigorous hikes near her mountain home. She showed Christlike love to the many visitors she hosted in her eclectic home, filled to the brim with treasures from her many travels, including her Chinese Chow dog, Wu, and her South American mimicking parrot, Loreeta. She also felt her testimony grow as she read great literature. She said, "I feel that the great spirit of literature is the spirit of God—that God has moved these people to write and speak as they have done . . . and that it is one of the ways of getting testimonies."

Ever the trailblazer, Maud was called to be the chaplain for the Utah state senate—the first woman called to the position in any state senate in the country. She carefully composed each prayer and delivered them in her compelling, sincere voice, a voice that changed four generations of students and the entire state of Utah.

Mei-Lin Liu

1972–
Taiwan

ONCE UPON A TIME, there was a little girl in Hualien, Taiwan, named Mei-Lin Liu. Whenever Mei-Lin saw someone get hurt, she was the first to run for a doctor. When the doctor arrived, Mei-Lin crouched next to the patient, eager to help.

Mei-Lin Liu's father owned an herbal shop, and her mother drove everywhere on her motorcycle to sell tea and vegetables. Mei-Lin's parents didn't expect her to continue her education after high school. They expected her to start working in the family store or find a husband.

As Mei-Lin grew up, she excelled in math, physics, and chemistry, and she decided to go to nursing school. Though hesitant at first, Mei-Lin Liu's parents supported her schooling. They were glad when she moved back home after working and studying in the big city to work in a local hospital. One day, Mei-Lin's co-worker at the hospital noticed that Mei-Lin was lonely and saddened by the trials in her life. She invited Mei-Lin to listen to the missionaries. "Maybe they can help you!" she said.

Everything the sister missionaries taught Mei-Lin brought her great joy. She asked the missionaries every day if there was an activity at the church that she could attend. She was baptized and a few years later served in the Taiwan Taichung Mission. As she taught the truths of the gospel, her own testimony grew from a few embers to a flame of faith. After her mission, she decided to attend Brigham Young University to study English. While in Utah, she earned her medical assistant degree from LDS Business College. Mei Lin was the first person in her family to earn a college degree.

At BYU, Mei-Lin Liu met her husband, and they became part of the Chinese branch in Salt Lake City. When Mei-Lin Liu became the Relief Society president she struggled with the language because the members spoke Mandarin, Cantonese, and English, but just like when she was a little girl, she was the first to respond when someone was in need, providing the healing blessings of sisterhood and the gospel.

Mere Mete Whaanga

1848–1944
New Zealand

ONCE UPON A TIME, there was a woman who was married to a chief. Her name was Mere, and she and her husband, Hirini, led an important Maori tribe in New Zealand known as the Ngati Kahungunu tribe. Mere and Hirini were loved by their tribe for their strong leadership and their humble hearts.

Fifteen years after Mere and Hirini were married, missionaries visited their city. When the missionaries raised their arms to bless their listeners, Mere gripped Hirini's hand. In the time of Hirini's grandfather, a spiritual leader of the Ngati Kahungnu tribe prophesied that the messengers of the true religion of the Maori would hail from the east and pray with their arms raised. Mere, Hirini, and hundreds of members of their tribe began listening to the missionaries and were baptized. Mere wrote of her baptism, "On coming out of the water, my heart was filled with love and understanding."

Mere and Hirini built an addition on their house for the missionaries, and Mere helped them feel at home while teaching them the Maori language. Some of the missionaries even called Mere their Maori mother. Through their leadership and relationship with their people, the Whaanga family built up the Church among the Ngati Kahungunu tribe. Mere and Hirini loved their tribe dearly, but their desire to be sealed in the temple grew each day. Eventually they made the difficult decision to leave their home and travel to Utah where the temple stood. They testified to their friends and family about the importance of temple blessings, and they gathered family names throughout New Zealand to take with them to the temple.

After a long journey by horseback, steamboat, ship, and train, the Whaanga family finally arrived in Salt Lake City. They were sealed in the temple and spent most of their time performing ordinances for their family members and the family members of their dear friends in New Zealand. After Hirini passed away, Mere was called on a mission to New Zealand. At sixty years old, she went to dozens of Latter-day Saint conferences on the North and South Islands. Mere's testimony and life experiences impacted hundreds of New Zealanders, including her family and members of the Ngati Kahungunu tribe. She had the power to "hold the people together with a little encouragement and advice."

Mere returned to Salt Lake at ninety years old. On her ninety-fifth birthday she gave a quilt to President Heber J. Grant as a birthday present. "But it's not my birthday!" said President Grant. "I know," said Mere. "It's mine!"

At ninety-six years old Mere passed away, leaving a pioneer legacy of stalwart faith that influenced many generations of her family and the Ngati Kahungunu tribe.

MINERVA TEICHERT

Minerva Teichert

1888–1976
United States

ONCE UPON A TIME, *there was a girl named Minerva who marveled at a fiery sunset from the porch of her family's ranch. Her father, an artistic man, pointed excitedly to each streak of orange, each purple cloud, and each crack of blue sky. Minerva gazed at the heavens and realized that God is the Master Artist who paints the sky to show His love for His children. In that moment, she felt a deep conviction that God could help her become an artist that spoke to people's souls and testified of God's love.*

Minerva had wanted to become an artist for as long as she could remember. At only three years old, she received her first paint set. She adored learning to mix colors, and before long she could paint barns and fields from her family's ranch. Minerva longed to gain professional training, but her family didn't have the means to send her to art school. Determined to find a way to attend art school, Minerva became a teacher. For three years she taught and saved her money, selling painted trinkets and small pictures until she finally had enough to attend the Art Institute of Chicago. She often came home from Chicago and helped on the ranch to earn money for the next semester. On one such visit, she met a quiet, friendly man named Herman. She liked him and they formed a close friendship, but she was focused on continuing her art training. Her success at the Art Institute of Chicago earned her a scholarship to the Art Students League in New York City. Minerva adored her teachers, who encouraged her to paint the history of the Latter-day Saints. Minerva felt the Spirit encourage this goal, and she felt especially inspired to highlight the role of women in the scriptures and in Church history.

On a visit home from New York, Herman proposed to Minerva and she accepted. They were married and moved to a Colorado ranch, where they raised five children. Minerva washed bottles for the dairy, fed chickens, planted and weeded fields, chopped wood, baked bread, and cared for her children. All the while, she painted on aprons, chopping blocks, and even the underside of the dining room table! She always carried a notebook with her to sketch her ideas for large murals. As her children grew up and Minerva found more time to paint, her ideas flowed from her sketchbook to her canvas. She painted Esther standing before the king, pioneer women bravely leading their children to Zion, Mary and Martha learning from the Savior, and many others. At age sixty she completed a mural at the Manti Utah Temple that spanned more than 4,000 square feet. It took only twenty-three days of work! Each day, before she and her assistant began painting, they prayed for inspiration and guidance. Each time she got stuck, she prayed again. She constantly invited the Lord into her painting and her life.

At the end of her long and accomplished life, Minerva gratefully recognized God's help in completing her mission as both an artist and as a mother. She said, "Art is my profession, and my children are my masterpieces."

NOELLE PIKUS-PACE

Noelle Pikus-Pace

1982–
United States

*O*NCE UPON A TIME, *there was a seventeen-year-old girl flying down an icy track head-first at ninety miles per hour. Her name was Noelle, and she fell in love with skeleton racing after her high school track coach gave her a sled and sent her down a track. She decided to dedicate her life to the sport with the hope of one day representing the United States at the Olympic games.*

A few years later, only 114 days away from the 2006 winter Olympics, Noelle was ranked first in the world in skeleton. Nothing could stand in the way of her dream of winning an Olympic medal. But one day during training, Noelle was caught on the track when a runaway bobsled careened into her. She was thrown twenty feet and severely broke her leg. Noelle's doctors told her she couldn't walk for two to three months and that she couldn't compete for at least a year. She felt defeated, until one day a doctor told her she could choose whether this injury would define her. Noelle wiped her tears and chose to move forward. She dedicated herself to physical therapy and recovery. Only three weeks later she was back on her sled, and the following year she won the world championships by the largest margin in the history of the sport.

As Noelle recovered and trained, she strove for balance in her life. She committed to reading the scriptures and praying every day. She cared for her young daughter and worked out in the basement while the baby slept. She played in a softball league with her husband and served in church callings. She focused on doing her best and not comparing herself with others. She said, "God does not expect us to be like someone else, or to compare ourselves with them. He expects us to have faith in Him, and He expects us to try." Eight years after the tragic accident that could have defeated her, Noelle flew down the track in her last race at the Sochi Winter Olympics on a sled built by her husband. At the end of the track, she saw her coach jumping up and down, and she knew she had won an Olympic medal. She bounded off the track and leaped into the stadium, where her husband and two children cheered and embraced her.

Noelle said, "Rise above it all, whatever holds you back, and become who you want to become."

Olga Kovářová Campora

1960–
Czech Republic

ONCE UPON A TIME, there was a little girl named Olga who lived in the Czech Republic and loved the absolute freedom of an open field more than almost anything else. When Olga visited her grandmother in the country, she raced through meadows and scrambled up trees with a stuffed monkey under her arm. The freedom Olga felt as she ran and climbed was quite different from the oppression of communism that she experienced in town and at school. Under communist rule, there were many strict laws, and people constantly worried about the secret police. People weren't allowed to talk publicly about God, and religious beliefs were ridiculed.

As Olga grew up, she hungered for truth. She sensed the deceitfulness of communist ideology and sought purpose for her life. She studied many philosophers and asked her friends if they felt the same way, but she was met with suspicion and negativity.

Olga's love of physical activity led her to study physical education. In college, she became interested in yoga. One day, Olga and her friend were invited by an older gentleman named Mr. Vojkůvka to his home to learn more about the practice of yoga. Olga felt a spirit in this man's home different from anything she had felt during communist lectures. Olga borrowed many yoga books from Mr. Vojkůvka's large library. As she read, she felt she was closer to finding a purpose for her life, and she desired greater direction and peace in her life. Eventually, Mr. Vojkůvka told Olga he was a member of The Church of Jesus Christ of Latter-day Saints. Over the next few months, Olga studied the gospel. One day, she read 2 Nephi 2:25: "Men are that they might have joy." Her heart was full to the brim with excitement. She had found the purpose and truth for which she had hungered!

To avoid the prying eyes of the secret police, Olga was baptized at midnight on a summer evening. After her baptism, Olga had a burning desire to share the gospel with others. However, preaching about God was very dangerous in the Czech Republic. Olga could be kicked out of school and sentenced to prison if she was caught. Mr. Vojkůvka suggested that Olga teach yoga classes to help people prepare to receive the gospel. After all, that is what prepared Olga.

Hundreds of people attended Olga's yoga classes and camps, where she taught physical health, the purpose of life, and how to build a life of service—all under the eye of the secret police. She helped countless Czechs take the first steps toward spirituality and belief in God. More than fifty young people she taught joined the Church, and some of them started their own yoga classes across the country.

Olga's undercover missionary work and yoga classes laid the foundation for missionary work in the Czech Republic.

the Otavaleñas Missionaries

UNKNOWN
Ecuador

ONCE UPON A TIME, in northern Ecuador, four sister missionaries navigated a busy market. Vibrant woven blankets and ponchos fluttered in the wind, and the lively chatter of hagglers and the smell of roasting meat floated through the aisles. The missionaries smiled and greeted the vendors and shoppers in the Otavalo market—one of the largest indigenous markets in Latin America.

Some of the market-goers stopped to stare at the missionaries, remarking to each other how young they looked. In Ecuador, it was customary for people to marry very young, so it was difficult to find sister missionaries who could serve at twenty-one years old. As a result, young women as young as fifteen years old were called to serve as full-time missionaries. One of these young sisters was named Ana Cumanda Rivera. She was baptized three years before her mission call in 1977 in Quito, Ecuador. Ana's first day in the mission field in Otavalo was spent hiding in a member's house from the people they wanted to teach—who were waiting for them with sticks and stones! On another day, Ana and her companion found themselves sprinting away from a stampede of cattle sent from a city that didn't want to hear their preaching.

Not long after these incidents, three Otavaleño sisters were called to serve with Ana. Ana helped the sisters memorize the discussions, and they helped Ana preach the gospel in Quichua, the most common language in Otavalo. The people in Otavalo began opening their doors and dropping their sticks and stones when the Otavaleño sisters joined Ana.

One of the Otavaleño sisters was named Luzmila Carrascal. Luzmila couldn't read or write, so each morning Ana gave literacy lessons after their scripture study. Ana hadn't taught literacy classes before, and she didn't know if she could help Luzmila. "Just teach me, and I will pray to Heavenly Father to help me understand what you teach me," Luzmila said. After a few months, Luzmila learned to read and write.

Luzmila had faith in the power of dreams. Ana and Luzmila were preparing to visit a family who was preparing for baptism in the Carabuela community when Luzmila said she had dreamed they should go to the Monserrat community instead. Ana suggested they pray, and they both felt Monserrat was the right choice. As they began the walk up to Monserrat, they saw the family from Carabuela walking toward them.

"Where are you going?" Luzmila asked.

"We are going to the chapel. We want to be baptized today!"

Ana and Luzmila shared an astonished glance, and together they walked to the chapel. The husband, wife, and nine-year-old son from Carabuela were baptized that day.

The Otavaleñas missionaries were young, but they were brave and faithful. Their service led many people to the gospel and changed their own lives forever.

Priscilla Sampson-davis

1927-2011
Ghana

ONCE UPON A TIME, there was a woman named Priscilla, but her students called her Samsi. Priscilla was a beloved art teacher at one of the best secondary schools for girls in Cape Coast, Ghana. Her students used to say "Samsie re ba oo!" which meant "Samsie's coming!" All the girls instantly straightened up. Priscilla was strict, but she loved teaching and she loved her students. She taught painting, drawing, jewelry making, and more. When students didn't have time in their schedules for art, Priscilla organized extra classes for them. She encouraged creative expression, and hundreds of students developed a passion for the arts because of her.

Priscilla was also one of the first members of the Church in Ghana. One day after sacrament meeting, she had a vision. She stood at the front of a chapel with a man dressed in white. Many people in the congregation bowed their heads.

"Why aren't those people joining in the singing?" the man asked her.

"Because they didn't go to school and they can't read English. They can't sing, and that is why they bow their heads," Priscilla said.

The messenger asked, "Wouldn't you like to help your sisters and brothers who can't read English and who can't join you in singing praises to Heavenly Father?"

Having taught and studied in English for so long, Priscilla didn't know the native language very well, but she said, "I will try."

The vision ended, and Priscilla immediately sat down with a pencil and paper and translated "Redeemer of Israel" into Fanti, the most common language in Ghana. She stared at the first verse, surprised at how easily it had come. A fire of inspiration burned in her as she translated the hymnbook and many missionary resources. Soon after she finished these translations, Priscilla felt prompted by the Holy Ghost to translate the Book of Mormon. As she translated, she heard a voice, almost like someone standing over her shoulder, saying, "No, not that word—use this instead." She knew the Lord was guiding her. When the translation was finished, she received a beautiful copy signed by the prophet, President David O. McKay. Priscilla fulfilled her mission to help her sisters and brothers learn and sing praises to their Heavenly Father.

REYNA ABURTO

Reyna I. Aburto

1963–
Nicaragua

ONCE UPON A TIME, on a dark night in Nicaragua just two days before Christmas, nine-year-old Reyna's house began to shake. After what felt like an eternity, the earthquake stopped. Reyna's house was in ruins, and her older brother had been killed.

In the days and weeks following the disaster, Reyna and her family mourned her brother and began rebuilding their life from the rubble in the city. Every day a truck drove through their neighborhood and gave Reyna's family food and water, and Reyna's cousins, aunts, and uncles took care of her and her parents. Reyna's heart filled with gratitude for the strangers and family members who had provided this relief to her family.

Six years later, Reyna and her family huddled together on a shared mattress in their living room and tried to sleep through the rumbling of distant explosions. Nicaragua was experiencing a violent revolution. Amid uncertainty and fear, Reyna's family held each other and hoped they would not be harmed.

When the revolution ended with the rebels overthrowing the government, it seemed like the whole country poured into the streets to celebrate. However, in the years following the revolution, the political conflicts in Nicaragua worsened. After finishing her degree in industrial engineering at the Universidad Centroamericana, Reyna and her family decided to immigrate to San Diego, where Reyna's extended family lived.

A few years after moving to San Diego, Reyna felt overwhelmed with her trials. She felt again that she was surrounded by ruins and rubble. Reyna's mother invited her to church with the missionaries who had been visiting her aunt, and Reyna decided to attend and seek relief. The moment she walked into The Church of Jesus Christ of Latter-day Saints, she felt peace and love. Every message seemed to be meant for her. She and her family were baptized, and the bishop asked Reyna to teach the Gospel Principles class at church. Carlos Aburto was one of the members of the class, and they quickly became best friends. A few years later they were married in the temple. Reyna started a translation business and spent many years watching lively World Cup soccer games with Carlos.

Through all the experiences of her life, Reyna learned that family was her most important possession, and she felt the impact of Christlike charity. Through the gospel of Jesus Christ, she gained peace in the knowledge that families are eternal and found many opportunities to serve others as she had been served. Reyna compares her life to a church in Germany that was rebuilt using many of the original burnt bricks after it was bombed in World War II. The pain and trials are there, but Christ has rebuilt it into something beautiful.

Rosemary Card

1989–
United States

ONCE UPON A TIME, there was a sixteen-year-old girl named Rosie walking in stilettos down a runway with lights blazing and cameras flashing. Rosie had moved to New York from Utah to pursue fashion modeling after constant bullying at school led her to consider a different path for her high school years.

Between the photo shoots and runways in New York, Milan, Singapore, and Tokyo, Rosie was living the dream. Rosie knew in her heart that this was part of her Heavenly Parents' plan for her, but she was puzzled. She thought living the glamorous lifestyle of an international model would bring her happiness and acceptance that still seemed out of reach. While she loved traveling the world and cherished her friendships with other models from many different countries, she eventually felt that she had more to give than a modeling career. She returned home to find her next purpose.

Rosie started attending Dixie State University and began to feel true happiness. When she succeeded in a class, helped a roommate with a problem, or created something new, she felt more joy than she had ever felt seeing her face on the pages of a magazine. She realized that the less she worried about how she looked to other people, the more creative and happy she felt.

Rosie considered a phrase she had heard often in her Young Women lessons: "Your body is a temple." The Spirit prompted Rosie to look deeper into this phrase, and she learned that temples aren't important because of the beautiful architecture or landscaping. Temples are important because of what happens *inside*, because they help us grow closer to Christ and fulfill our purpose. This is the same reason our bodies are important. Using social media, Rosie shouted this message from the rooftops.

The temple had always been dear to Rosie's heart. During a particularly difficult period in her modeling career in Tokyo, Rosie visited the temple often to gain peace and strength. A few years after she graduated college, Rosie again sought peace and direction as she considered a career change. As Rosie pondered and listened for the Spirit, an impression popped into her mind. "I wish someone would make cute and comfy temple dresses. . . . Why don't I make cute and comfy temple dresses?" Without any experience in clothing manufacturing or business ownership, Rosie set out to follow the prompting she had received. After a year of hard work and at the end of her savings, news of Rosie's new line of simple, beautiful, and comfortable dresses spread throughout the United States. After the *New York Times* featured Rosie's story, she received orders from around the world. As her business, Q.NOOR, grows, Rosie continues to raise her voice about the divine roles of women as creators, leaders, and disciples of Christ. Her message is simple: The most important thing for a woman to do in this life is whatever her Heavenly Parents call her to do.

Sahar Qumsiyeh

1971–
Palestine

ONCE UPON A TIME, *there was a woman named Sahar scrambling up a ten-foot wall on the outskirts of Jerusalem while the footfalls of armed Israeli soldiers grew louder behind her. Sahar reached the top of the wall just as the soldiers rounded the corner. She dropped to the other side of the wall and squeezed through a hole in a wire fence and out of sight. She traveled through dusty Jerusalem roads until she arrived at her destination. Peace enveloped her, and she breathed a sigh of relief as she entered the chapel of the BYU Jerusalem Center. Today Sahar was teaching Sunday School, and she offered a prayer of gratitude that she had safely made it to church once again.*

Sahar's life hadn't always been so perilous. Long before she climbed walls to escape soldiers, Sahar was a little girl climbing smooth white rocks and gathering poppies in the hills near Bethlehem where angels announced the Savior's birth to shepherds 2,000 years ago. Sahar was a Palestinian, and she spent sunny childhood days splashing in the Red Sea or visiting the natural springs near the Dead Sea.

As the years passed, tensions between Israeli soldiers and Palestinians escalated near Sahar's home in Bethlehem. Sahar struggled to focus on her high school studies as the sound of rifles echoed through her neighborhood. Her nose and eyes often stung with tear gas from protests near her school, and she saw neighbors lose their homes, their businesses, and even their lives. Sahar was devastated by the violence that surrounded her, and she concluded that God must hate her and her people, the Palestinians. It was impossible to imagine what peace might feel like with the chaos around her.

Nevertheless, Sahar dedicated herself to her studies. Sahar earned her master's degree in statistics from Brigham Young University, despite receiving a scholarship offer four times as large from a university in Washington DC. Each time she had begun the process to reject the smaller BYU offer, she had known deep down it was where she was meant to be. While attending BYU, Sahar became curious about the Church and asked her friend Shae to tell her more. As Shae explained the gospel and the plan of salvation, Sahar thought "it was as though Shae were putting all the pieces of a puzzle together, and for the first time [she] could see the beautiful picture." Sahar was baptized in 1996, despite strong opposition from her family.

When Sahar finished her master's degree, she returned to Palestine. Even though the situation in her country was the same as she had left it, she felt a new peace envelop her. She knew now that God loved her and her people.

This knowledge helped Sahar as she began the daunting task of attending church every Sabbath. Palestinians living in the West Bank were not allowed into Jerusalem where church services were held, so Sahar had to sneak in. The dangerous journey each week often took more than three hours, but Sahar braved bumpy hot taxi rides, treks up steep hills, and the fear of Israeli soldiers for twelve years to worship with fellow Saints.

Sahar received her PhD in statistics and moved to Idaho to teach mathematics at a university, but she is often reminded of how the Savior walked with her on both peaceful and dangerous days in the city of His birth. Sahar said, "My country has never experienced peace, but now I feel my heart has enough peace to cover the entire country of Palestine."

Sveinbjörg Guðmundsdóttir

1929–
Iceland

ONCE UPON A TIME, a woman named Sveinbjörg heard a knock on her door in Reykjavic, Iceland. On her doorstep were two church employees with a once-in-a-lifetime opportunity. The men explained to Sveinbjörg that the missionaries in Iceland were in desperate need of an Icelandic translation of the Book of Mormon. Without hesitation, Sveinbjörg accepted the translation job and quit her job as a secretary for the biggest firm in Iceland.

Sveinbjörg didn't feel qualified to translate on her own, so she found another man, a kind doctor and linguist, to help. However, after two and a half years, only 1 and 2 Nephi had been translated. The missionaries needed the Book of Mormon, and they needed it badly. They suggested that Sveinbjörg translate an abridged version of the scriptures, which would include the most important passages for missionary teaching. As Sveinbjörg fed the paper into her typewriter to write her approval for this new plan, she froze. Something felt wrong. She knelt in her office near the window and asked God what He wanted her to do. As she prayed, the calm voice of the Spirit cut through the noisy passing cars and said, "Do not worry, my child, the translation of the Book of Mormon will be finished this year if you are willing to work hard."

Sveinbjörg took a deep breath and wrote a letter to Church headquarters. She couldn't approve of the new plan because it wasn't what God wanted. She promised that the translation would be done by the end of the year. She gazed at the letter and thought, "What on earth am I doing? This is impossible."

But Sveinbjörg trusted God's promise. She and the doctor split the translation of the rest of the Book of Mormon. Through her faith and willingness to work hard, she finished translating the last verses on December 30, 1979. Sveinbjörg didn't want the experience to end. She said, "It was so wonderful to work on the word of God."

thi thu ha

UNKNOWN
Vietnam

ONCE UPON A TIME, *Once upon a time there was a young woman zipping through a bustling street on her brother's motor scooter. Hundreds of thousands of young people arrive in Ho Chi Minh City, Vietnam, each year searching for work. Thi Thu Ha was one of these young people. She smiled her gentle smile, and the wind whipped her hair as she drove past entire families huddled on single motorcycles, students on their way to school, and market salespeople with their wares balanced precariously on the back of their bikes.*

Thi Thu Ha slowed and parked her brother's scooter outside a shop. When she exited the shop a few minutes later she froze, her stomach dropping to her shoes. Her brother's bike was gone! Thi Thu Ha stared up and down the street, willing her brother's bike to come into view, but she knew the thief was long gone. Her shoulders sagged, and she began the long walk home.

When Thi Thu Ha was baptized at the age of twenty-one, she promised herself she would become a full time missionary. After months of saving every Vietnamese dong she could, she had finally saved enough money for a mission. But now she had to pay her brother for the stolen bike. She was disappointed, but she began the process of saving her money again.

Only a short time later, Thi Thu Ha lost her job. She began cleaning houses to make money, but she was only able to save a little money each month. It would take years to save enough money for a mission. She fasted for two days, pleading for help and guidance. At the end of her fast, she felt the warmth of the Spirit, and she knew that her Heavenly Parents were proud of her for striving to serve a mission. The next day, she woke up with the strength and resolve she needed to find a new job. After a few months, she had saved the required amount again, but when she came home one day, the money was gone from the hiding place in her apartment! Her heart sank, but she remembered the warm feeling of the Spirit, and she started the process of working and saving again. To Thi Thu Ha's dismay, her money was stolen a third time, but still the warm feeling carried her forward.

The fourth time Thi Thu Ha saved up the money for her mission, she finally met with the mission president to turn in her missionary application. She wept as she told him how hard she had worked for this opportunity and how much she loved the Lord and wanted to serve Him. Sister Ha saved enough money for four missions, and she served with the strength of four missionaries. Whenever she felt discouraged, she remembered the warmth of the Spirit. She was confident in her Heavenly Parents' love for her, and it gave her the strength to overcome her challenges.

Tina Haskin Reisner

1992–
United States

ONCE UPON A TIME, there was a girl named Tina crouching in front of her team's goal. Her ears strained to hear the telltale sound of bells jingling in the basketball-sized rubber ball that would soon careen toward her side of the court. Her opponent hurled the ball toward her, and Tina slid onto her side at the same time as her two teammates. Tina smiled as she heard the satisfying thump of the ball colliding with her teammate's leg—she had blocked the goal.

Her teammate then tossed the ball to Tina, who tapped the goalpost behind her to orient herself, wound up, and released the ball with all her might. It rolled across the court, and Tina held her breath until she heard the referee blow two short blasts on his whistle. Tina had scored a goal! She hugged her teammates and together they crouched again, ready for their opponents' next attack.

Tina was captain of her high school's goalball team, the most popular team sport for the blind and visually impaired. Tina was born prematurely, and her retinas hadn't fully developed, leaving her blind from birth. She was adopted from New Dehli, India, when she was a baby and grew up in Chicago. She loved to read, play outside, and climb trees like the other children in her neighborhood, but she often felt that people didn't know how to include her at school and in church. Nevertheless, Tina faithfully studied the scriptures, attended the temple, and served as a Young Women class president.

When Tina began her university studies, she found friends and a community who supported her and saw her for the person she was, not for her blindness. She served a Church service mission, where she set up web pages and forums for blind and visually impaired members of the Church to share resources and their testimonies. As a graduate student, she taught classes for the English department of her university, spoke at conferences for Guiding Eyes for the Blind, an organization that advocates for blind people and seeing eye dogs, and served in various callings in her ward.

Tina continues to advocate for blind people and service animals while also teaching at a high school for the deaf and blind. She encourages other people with vision disabilities: "Your only limits are those you think internally about yourself. . . . Blindness should not be the thing that holds you back from pursuing a college degree, a marriage, or a career you love. . . . That should be the last thing that limits you. You can do things you put your mind to and use imagination and determination."

Tsune Ishida Nachie

1856–1938
Japan

*O*NCE UPON A TIME, *there was a twenty-two-year-old mission president in Tokyo, Japan, showing his newly hired forty-nine-year-old housekeeper how to sweep and dust the mission home. Tsune Nachie, who had been a housekeeper in high-profile Western businessmen's homes for many decades, watched him, amused.*

In reality, Tsune's normal salary was far higher than the missionaries could afford, but when she had taken her nieces to the Sunday School classes for Japanese children of all faiths that the missionaries held in Tokyo, she was intrigued. Eager to learn more about The Church of Jesus Christ of Latter-day Saints, she accepted the job offer in the mission home without revealing her interest in the Church. As Tsune prepared meals, she listened carefully to the missionaries' conversations and lessons. Tsune surprised the elders when she declared she had a testimony of the gospel and wanted to be baptized. After the elders suggested Tsune needed to study the gospel more before her baptism, she called the minister of the church she had been attending and informed him that she was joining a new church. She returned to the missionaries and insisted she was ready to be baptized. The missionaries were impressed by her boldness, and a few weeks later they baptized Tsune in a stream.

From that day forward, Tsune became both a fearless missionary and a second mother to the elders in the mission. Tsune invited friends to stay with her at the mission home, where she taught them truths from the Book of Mormon and helped them choose to be baptized. She testified to the parents at the children's Sunday School that the gospel would bless their lives. Knowing how homesick the missionaries could be during the winter holidays, Tsune cooked turkey dinners to help them feel at home. When one desperately homesick missionary craved a breakfast recipe he loved from home, Tsune traveled by train to deliver the food to the missionary and teach him how to prepare it just as his mother had.

As Tsune reached retirement years, the missionaries she had loved and served raised money to fund Tsune's immigration to Hawaii. There, she could finally enter the Laie Hawaii Temple to perform ordinances for herself and the long list of ancestors she had collected since her baptism so many years before. On June 5, 1924, Tsune became the first Japanese member of the Church to enter the temple. When asked by a census worker in Hawaii about her occupation, Tsune responded that she was a missionary. Nearly every day, she traveled among the Japanese people in Hawaii to preach the gospel. When she first arrived, there were no missionaries assigned to teach Japanese people on the island. In the fifteen years before she passed away, she lived to see the organization of a branch of Japanese members and a Japanese-speaking mission in Hawaii. The mission president in Hawaii said of Tsune, "My first impression was not unlike the lasting impression carried to the tops of the mountains by those who have felt the force of her great spirit and the tenderness of her love— [she is] like a jewel, small in size but most precious."

Vaikato tāvutu

UNKNOWN
Tonga

ONCE UPON A TIME, there was a 102-year-old woman hauling sharp, heavy coral bricks at a construction site in Tonga. "Vaikato!" the building supervisor scolded. He didn't like it when she exerted herself so much, but she was unstoppable. She arrived at the building site before anyone else each morning, and when the other building missionaries slowed in the hot sun, she encouraged them to keep working.

"At least take these gloves, Vaikato. Your hands are bleeding!" he said.

"The Savior's hands bled for me, and I am not ashamed to have my hands bleed for the Savior's work," she answered with a glowing smile.

The building supervisor often saw Vaikato pause in her work with tears streaming down her wrinkled cheeks and weathered hands raised in a prayer of gratitude. The church building that would be erected on this site was the fulfillment of a vision Vaikato had received many years earlier. At the time, she had been very ill and serving as the Relief Society president on the island of 'Uiha. She asked the apostle, George Albert Smith, who was visiting the island, to give her a blessing. He promised her that if she lived faithfully, she would see a chapel built on her island. As he spoke, she saw the chapel in a beautiful vision. For years, she shared her vision with her friends and other members of the Church, but each passing year without a chapel brought more ridicule. Despite her friends' disbelief, Vaikato never doubted that her vision would become a reality.

When the Church finally sent Tongan missionaries with building plans to 'Uiha, Vaikato described to them in detail the building layout. The missionaries were astonished and asked her if she had seen the plans. She answered that she had seen them in a vision, complete with a gold steeple. "Ah, there you are a bit mistaken," they said. "These plans call for a silver steeple." However, the silver steeple that was meant for 'Uiha was unexpectedly diverted to a different island, and they received another steeple in its place made of bronze that shone like gold in the sun.

The chapel was nearly completed, and Vaikato stood in front of the beautiful building, radiating joy. She said, "I know now how relieved Joseph Smith felt when the Lord provided witnesses to the Book of Mormon. The Lord has provided a witness to the whole island to the truth of my vision from so many years ago."

Albright, Mark. "The Gladys Knight Conversion Story," *LDS Magaⅈ ne*, Jan. 21 2013.

latterdaysaintmag.com/article-1-12092/.

"An Inspired, Timely Translation." The Church of Jesus Christ of Latter-day Saints. https://www.churchofjesuschrist.org/study/history/global-histories/iceland/stories-of-faith/is-05-an-inspired-timely-translation?lang=eng.

Armstrong, Jamie. "How Gladys Knight Became a Latter-day Saint." *LDS Living*, Feb. 5, 2019.

www.ldsliving.com/How-Gladys-Knight-Became-a-Mormon/s/76709.

Arrington, H. H. "Babcock, Maud May." Accessed Dec. 08, 2020.

https://www.encyclopedia.com/women/encyclopedias-almanacs-transcripts-and-maps/babcock-maud-may-1867-1954

Asioli, Laura. Interview by Annette Pimentel. "An Advocate of Faith," The Mormon Women Project, 18 Apr., 2014.

https://www.mormonwomen.com/interview/an-advocate-of-faith/.

"Autobiography of Mary E. Lightner (1818–1913)." Book of Abraham Project.

http://www.boap.org/LDS/Early-Saints/MLightner.html.

Bancroft, Kaitlyn, and Davis Clipper. "UVU's First Female President Shows 'Dreams Are Free'."

The Daily Universe, 26 Sept. 2018.

universe.byu.edu/2018/09/21/uvus-first-female-president-shows-dreams-are-free-1/.

Bates, Emily, guest. "Searching for Truth, in Science and Faith."

The Mormon Women Project Podcast, Apr. 28, 2019. https://www.mormonwomen.com/2019/04/ podcast-searching-for-truth-in-science-and-faith/.

Black, Susan Easton and Mary Jane Woodger. *Women of Character: Profiles of 100 Prominent LDS Women*. American Fork, UT: Covenant Communications, 2011, 90–93, 285–288, 292–294.

"Break the Soil of Bitterness," YouTube video. LDS Church History, Mar. 8, 2017.

https://www.youtube.com/watch?v=7epPr-75Fu0U

Burger, David. "Benefit for New Endowed Scholarship at Dixie State for Utahn Who Was Polish Resistance Fighter during Nazi Occupation," *The Salt Lake Tribune*, Aug. 11, 2011.

https://archive.sltrib.com/article.php?id=52390586&itype=cmsid.

Campora Olga Kovářová. *Saint Behind Enemy Lines*. Salt Lake City: Deseret Book, 1997.

Cannon, Elaine and Shirley A. Teichert. *Minerva! The Story of an Artist with a Mission*.

Salt Lake City: Bookcraft, 1997.

Card, Rosemary. Interview by Lydia Defranchi, "Dressed Like A Queen."

The Mormon Women Project, June 2, 2016. https://www.mormonwomen.com/interview/dressed-like-queen/.

Card, Rosemary. *Model Mormon: Fighting for Self-Worth on the Runway* and as an Independent Woman. Springville, Utah: Cedar Fort, Inc., 2018.

Caroline Kwok interview: Kowloon Tong, Hong Kong, Oct. 26, 2001. Transcript,Church History Library. Accessed Nov. 10, 2020. https://catalog.churchofjesuschrist.org/record?id=be1c41f1-cf88-4663-b29c-fb23cf-f2e2c3&view=browse.

"Celebration of life: Mrs. Priscilla Sampson-Davis, aged 84," Church History Catalog. Accessed Oct. 17, 2019.

https://catalog.churchofjesuschrist.org/record?id=a1aadd8f-6ee9-427d-a4dc-08bb-6414d109&view=summary.

"Dr. Astrid S. Tuminez: Shaped by the Power of Education." *Diverse*, Mar. 22, 2019.

https://diverseeducation.com/article/141156/.

"Ensure Independence of Judiciary, New Chief Judge Tells Obaseki," Jan. 26, 2017.

thenationonlineng.net/ensure-independence-judiciary-new-chief-judge-tells-obaseki/.

"'God Is Just,' Says Chief Judge Ikponmwen." *News*, Feb. 21, 2017,

news-ng.churchofjesuschrist.org/article/god-is-just-says-chief-judge-ikponmwen.

Gong, S. "Branch Builder in Vietnam." Accessed Nov. 17, 2020.

https://history.churchofjesuschrist.org/article/sister-stories-faithful-sister-thi-thu-ha?lang=eng.

Guðmundsdóttir, Sveinbjörg. Interview by Kristen Edwards.

"To Work on the Word of God." The Mormon Women Project, Sept. 18, 2018. https://www.mormonwomen.com /interview/ to-work-on-the-word-of-god/.

Haskin, Tina. Tina Haskin interview: Salt Lake City, Utah, 21 Aug. 2015,

https://catalog.churchofjesuschrist.org/record?id=fa53b6a9-ce8e-4baa-b507-bb2914d-d16a3&view=summary.

Hill, N. C. "Never Alone in Sierra Leone," *Liahona*, Sept. 2015.

Historias SUD: Relato de Ana Cumandá Rivera: IglesiaJesucristoSud.org. (n.d.) Accessed Oct. 17, 2020. https://sudamericanoroeste.laiglesiadejesucristo.org/historiadelaiglesia/ecuador/fe/relato-de-ana-cumanda.

Ikponmwen, Esohe Frances. Oral History, 14 Feb. 2017.

https://catalog.churchofjesuschrist.org/assets?id=5bd4707d-5df2-428f-90fb-c650314097ae&crate=0&index=0.

"Interviews with African Americans in Utah, Lucille Bankhead, Interview 1,"

Interview by 1030292511 790084409 L. G. Kelen, Nov. 18, 2018. https://collections.lib.utah.edu/ark:/87278/s6836026

Interview with Juana B. Zuniga by Irene Zuniga, 1976, "Interview no. 253," Institute of Oral History, University of Texas at El Paso.

Iverson, S. J. "Chile," *Ensign*, Feb. 1977.

https://www.churchofjesuschrist.org/study/ensign/1977/02/chile?lang=eng

Kramer, Lyneve Wilson and Eva Durrant Wilson. "Mary Isabella Hales Horne,"

Faithful Sister and Leader, Aug. 1982. https://www.churchofjesuschrist.org/study/ensign/1982/08/mary-isabella-hales-horne-faithful-sister-and-leader?lang=eng.

Larsen, Sonia. "Golfers for Good." LDS Living, Apr. 9, 2010, http://www.ldsliving.com/Golfers-for-Good/s/3977.

LeBaron, Elwin Dale.

"Pioneer sisters in Africa: women of courage and faith: the LDS Relief Society and Mormon Women : Cross-disciplinary Considerations Conference."

Provo, Utah: Women's Research Institute, Brigham Young University, 1992. Accessed Oct. 17, 2019. https://catalog.churchofjesuschrist.org/record?id=02db43ff-9f3b-425d-981f-adde5366f1b7&view=summary.

"Lidia Zakrzewski and the Chicago Polish Branch."

The Church of Jesus Christ of Latter-day Saints, https://www.churchofjesuschrist.org/study/history/global-histories/poland/stories-of-faith/pl-06-lidia-zakrzewski-and-the-chicago-polish-branch-bb?lang=eng.

"Lidia Zakrzewski," *Daily Herald*,

Mar. 29, 2011. https://www.heraldextra.com/lifestyles/announcements/obituaries/lidia-zakrzewski/article_032307e0-7e9a-5b88-84f5-69184910ad3c.html.

Liu, Mei-Lin. Mei-Lin Liu interview: Draper, Utah. Nov. 14 , 2003.

https://catalog.churchofjesuschrist.org/record?id=1c563760-c11d-451f-8f15-9f956750c7ea&view=summary.

Lundgreen, Cecilie. Interview by Eline Amundson. "The Lord Really is Kind," The Mormon Women Project, July 11, 2017. https://www.mormonwomen.com/interview/7815/.

Manea, Claire T. Oral History. Interview by R. Lanier Britsch. Papeete Tahiti Nui, French Polynesia, 1974. Typescript. The James Moyle Oral History Program, Archives, Historical Department of The Church of Jesus Christ of Latter-day Saints, Salt Lake City, Utah.

"Maori Tribal Leader, 90, To Live Here." Newspapers.com, *The Salt Lake Tribune*, Nov. 14,

> 1938. www.newspapers.com/clip/7260343/the-salt-lake-tribune/.

Mavimbela, Julia Nompi 1917–2000. Julia N. Mavimbela interview. Accessed Aug. 3, 2020.

> https://catalog.churchofjesuschrist.org/assets?id=87be2596-4a34-43c0-9955-b3a5b7e01af1&crate=0&index=0.

Mitchell, T. "Lucille Bankhead." Accessed November 04, 2020.

> https://www.utahwomenshistory.org/bios/lucille-bankhead/.

"'My Heart Was Filled with . . . Understanding.'" The Church of Jesus Christ of Latter-day Saints,

> www.churchofjesuschrist.org/study/history/global-histories/new-zealand/stories-of-faith/nz-02-my-heart-was-filled-with-understanding?lang=eng.

Nixon, Kelsey. *Kitchen Confidence*. Clarkson Potter/Publishers: 2014.

"Our Story." Kelsey Nixon, Jan. 27, 2018. https://www.kelseynixon.com/our-story/.

Parshall, Ardis E. "Edith Russell: Associate Editor, I Was There." *Keepapitchinin*, The Mormon History Blog, June 11, 2017. www.keepapitchinin.org/2017/06/11/edith-russell-associate-editor-17/.

Pikus-Pace, Noelle. *Focused: Keeping Your Life on Track, One Choice at a Time*. Salt Lake City: Deseret Book, 2014.

Pinborough, J. U. and B. J. Clarke. "Florence Chukwurah: The Miracle of Change," *Ensign*, June 1996.

Prince, Gregory A. "'There Is Always a Struggle': An Interview with Chieko N. Okazaki." *Dialogue: A Journal of Mormon Thought*, vol. 45, no. 1, 2012, 114–140. https://www.dialoguejournal.com/wpcontent/uploads/sbi/articles/Dialogue_V45N01_CO.pdf.

Qumsiyeh, Sahar. *Peace for a Palestinian: One Woman's Story of Faith amidst War in the Holy Land*. Salt

Lake City: Deseret Book, 2018.

Reeder, Jennifer and Kate Holbrook. *At the Pulpit: 185 Years of Discourses by Latter-day Saint Women*, The Church Historians Press, 2017, 253–58.

"Reeve Nield Player Profile." <u>SA Women's Golf</u>, Mar. 2008, 9–10.

"Reyna Aburto's Story—Part 1: Heartbreak and Hope," YouTube, uploaded by The Church of Jesus Christ of Latter-day Saints, July 19, 2018. https://www.youtube.com/watch?v=FG9b3JnwZ74.

"Reyna Aburto's Story—Part 2: A Difficult Journey," YouTube, uploaded by The Church of Jesus Christ of Latter-day Saints, July 19, 2018. https://www.youtube.com/watch?v=JQih5f_Cg20.

"Reyna Aburto's Story—Part 3: A New Beginning," YouTube, uploaded by The Church of Jesus Christ of Latter-day Saints, July 19, 2018, https://www.youtube.com/watch?v=JQih5f_Cg20.

Ricks, K. (n.d.). "Pearls of the Orient," *Ensign*, Sept. 1991.

> https://www.churchofjesuschrist.org/study/ensign/1991/09/pearls-of-the-orient?lang=eng.

Russell, Edith. "But My Dear, A Woman!" *The Improvement Era*, Mar. 1945, 148–49.

Russell, Edith. "The Russells Did Not Go To Church—Chapter 3." *The Relief Society Magazine*, Oct. 1948, 671–74.

Russell, Edith. "What Is Man?" *The Improvement Era*, Sept. 1945, 528–29.

Saints: The Story of the Church of Jesus Christ in the Latter Days. Vol. 1. The Church of Jesus Christ of Latter-day Saints, 2018, 5–8, 31–32, 121–23, 221–22, 470, 543–44.

Sitati, Gladys Nangoni. "Gladys N., Sitati interview." Accessed Apr. 30, 2020.

> https://catalog.churchofjesuschrist.org/assets?id=d9fef68e-bdb8-4b67-8196-c0693a-83ca3d&crate=0&index=0.

"Spotlight Series: Kelsey Nixon."

> NORMONS, Sept. 26, 2016, https://www.normons.com/spotlight-series-kelsey-nixon/.

Stack, Peggy Fletcher. "Beloved Mormon Women's Leader Chieko Okazaki Dies," *The Salt Lake Tribune*, Aug. 5, 2011, archive.sltrib.com/article.

php?id=52320992&itype=cmsid.

Stevenson, Aïda. Interview by Lydia Defranchi. Translation provided by Haleigh Heaps Burgon. "A Life in Full Color," The Mormon Women Project, Mar. 17, 2016.

>https://www.mormonwomen.com/interview/a-life-in-full-color/.

Swensen, Jason. "How a Latter-day Saint Convert from 'the Slums' Became Utah Valley University's First Female President," Church News and Events, Apr. 3, 2019.

>www.churchofjesuschrist.org/church/news/how-a-latter-day-saint-convert-from-the-

>slums-became-utah-valley-universitys-first-female-president?lang=eng.

"Tina's walk of life," *Liberalis*, Summer 2017, 10–11.

>https://issuu.com/usudigitalcommons/docs/liberalis_summer_2017.

Tuminez, Astrid. "Dare to . . . Empower and be Empowered," *TEDx ChiangMai*, Mar. 2, 2016.

>https://www.youtube.com/watch?v=w_6AWy0g56Y.

Tuminez, Astrid. "Education Carves Path From Manila to Microsoft." *Women and Girls, News Deeply*, Oct. 26, 2017.

>www.newsdeeply.com/womenand-girls/articles/2016/05/23/education-carves-path-from-manila-to-microsoft.

"The Lord Vindicates Vaikato." The Church of Jesus Christ of Latter-day Saints, www.churchofjesuschrist.org/study/history/global-histories/tonga/stories-of-faith/to-04-the-lord-vindicates-vaikato?lang=eng.

"The Ultimate Bucket List | Hope Works," YouTube, uploaded by The Church of Jesus Christ of Latter-day Saints, Nov. 11, 2019,

>https://www.youtube.com/watch?v=dzbbxhZsyuE.

"'There Must Be Something There.'" The Church of Jesus Christ of Latter-day Saints.

>www.churchofjesuschrist.org/study/history/global-histories/nigeria/stories-of-faith/ng-04-there-must-be-something-there?lang=eng.

Turley, Richard E. and Brittany Chapman Nash. *Women of Faith in the Latter Days*. Vol. 2.Salt Lake City: Deseret Book, 2012.

_____. Women of Faith in the Latter Days. Vol. 3. Salt Lake City: Deseret Book, 2014.

_____. *Women of Faith in the Latter Days*. Vol. 4. Salt Lake City: Deseret Book, 2017.

Valenzuela, Maria Teresa Toro. "Threads of Faith," interview by Jenny Willmore. The Mormon Women Project, Sept. 4, 2018.

>https://www.mormonwomen.com/interview/threads-of-faith/

Van Leer, T. (1997, February 11). "Lucille not Afraid to Speak Her Mind."

>https://www.deseret.com/1997/2/11/19294581/lucille-not-afraid-to-speak-her-mind.

Watkins, N. "Maud May Babcock." Accessed Dec. 8, 2020.

>https://www.utahwomenshistory.org/bios/maud-may-babcock/.

About the Artists

Brooke Browen has loved to create since she was young. She attended BYU before continuing her art education independently. She now lives in the shadows of the mountains of Utah raising her four boys with an enthusiasm for creating.

Esther Hi'ilani Candari is primarily figurative artist and often explores the nuance of human culture, experience, and psychology that can be expressed through portraiture. Much of her work draws upon her experiences growing up in Hawai'i in a mixed race household. She has an BFA from BYU-H, an MFA from Liberty University, has studied at the New York Academy of Art, and interned with Joseph Brickey. Currently, she lives in Utah County with her husband, two rescue dogs, and an ever-growing collection of houseplants.

Sarah Hawkes is currently in the Bachelor of Fine Arts program for illustration at Brigham Young University, and believes the best children's books are for adults and children alike. She is passionate about religious fine art and bright and uplifting children's book illustration. Sarah loves to work in a variety of mediums and has worked on projects of all kinds; from murals to apparel to home decor. When not working on commissions or original work, Sarah loves Indian food, road trips, and long hikes.

Victoria-Riza Hyde is an artist and illustrator who specializes in fashion, beauty, and portraiture. Layering watercolor and gouache to create depth and texture, she creates works that showcase beauty diversity. Victoria-Riza founded The Riza, a blog that accompanies her multi-creative works with conversations on diversity, culture, race, and other social issues, especially in regards to art and the fashion industry. She also shares her creative journey and creative process to inspire the creative community. Her work has been seen in *Vanity Fair UK* and she has worked with clients such as *Pacificus Magazine*, New American Economy, Alt Summit, *Arab-American Psycho*, and The House that Lars Built.

Samantha Long is a an artist who loves patterns, bright colors, and whimsy. She grew up in Utah Valley with her left-brained accountant mother and her right-brained musician father. She therefore states that her brain is equally balanced. She started taking art lessons at the age of 10 with fine artist Monique DeWitt then went on to study Illustration at Brigham Young University. Samantha currently lives in American Fork, Utah with an empty guinea pig cage, an orderly yarn drawer sorted by color, and several underperforming plants.

Brookynne Noe is a Nashville-based artist/illustrator and mother. She loves creating images that tell stories about motherhood and womanhood. When she's not drawing, she's usually discussing her latest fantasy read or hoping her four year old doesn't find her hidden stash of cookies.

Ellie Osborne is one of the world's top bird enthusiasts and she hunts for tiny flowers amongst weeds every spring. The little things are everything to Ellie, and she wants to draw attention to the beauty found in the details of the world. From its creatures to its stories and the people who create them, she wants to celebrate them all. Ellie graduated from Brigham Young University with a BFA in Illustration, and she is passionate about learning outside of school too. She loves to travel and discover new places, with Italy being her favorite place, but calls Utah home.

About the Author

WHEN RAELEIGH WILKINSON was a preschooler, her uncle found her in furious tears because her cousins told her "only boys can be doctors". Although Raeleigh turned out to be far too squeamish to pursue a career in medicine, she always carried her stubborn conviction that girls can do anything. Raeleigh studied mechanical engineering, and she has worked on robots, rockets, and roller coasters. Raeleigh is a lifelong book lover, and has been gobbling up stories like marshmallow yams at Thanksgiving dinner for as long as she can remember. She loves long walks to the park with her husband and two children, stealing time to write stories during nap time, and spending far too much time in bakeries. *Bedtime Stories for Girls of Destiny* is her first book.